HOW TO DO EVERYTHING
from The Man Who Should Know

HOW TO DO EVERYTHING

FROM THE MAN WHO SHOULD KNOW

RED GREEN

A Completely Exhaustive Guide to
Do-it-Yourself and Self-help

Anchor Canada

Copyright © 2010 Steve Smith
Anchor Canada edition published 2011

All rights reserved. The use of any part of this publication, reproduced, transmitted
in any form or by any means electronic, mechanical, photocopying, recording or
otherwise, or stored in a retrieval system without the prior written consent of the
publisher—or, in the case of photocopying or other reprographic copying, a license from
the Canadian Copyright Licensing Agency—is an infringement of the copyright law.

Anchor Canada is a registered trademark.

Library and Archives Canada Cataloguing in Publication is available upon request.

ISBN 978-0-385-66775-3

Book design: Leah Springate

Printed and bound in the USA

Published in Canada by
Anchor Canada, a division of
Random House of Canada Limited

Visit Random House of Canada Limited's website: www.randomhouse.ca

10   9   8   7   6   5   4   3   2   1

CONTENTS:

INTRODUCTION

A long time ago in Europe, there was a renaissance. I think it was during the Industrial Age. And out of that period came what they call a Renaissance Man—a person who was respected for the scope rather than the depth of his expertise. Unfortunately, all of that has changed, and these days a Renaissance Man is just a guy who meets women at fancy hotels.

In fact, for the last fifty years there has been a strong movement towards specialization. They've been telling us all that if you want to be successful, you're better off to know a whole lot about something than a little bit about everything. This has been a huge mistake, along with computers, the new Coke and hair weaves.

I blame Science. The scientific community has used its knowledge of various specialized fields to make the rest of us feel like the morons we may or may not be. The truth is that in most situations there is nothing more useless than a scientific expert. Usually, the genius who runs a particle accelerator has no idea how to unclog a toilet, even though the two are very similar challenges. Likewise, being the world's foremost expert on arachnids does not make you an interesting dinner conversationalist, especially if something just moved in the salad.

So this book is an attempt to get back to the days when every man had a toolbox and would fearlessly attack whatever challenge confronted him. There is no downside to this approach. If you succeed in fixing the problem, you gain a sense of accomplishment and self-reliance and are ready for the next obstacle.

If you fail, you are willing to pay an expert without suspicion or remorse.

It's a DIY book, it's a self-help book, it's an environmental action plan. Like fertilizer, it may be spread thinly over many fields, but you know it's there. If you're looking to handle drips in your bathroom or in your personal life, or simply to end global warming—or the discussion of it—look no further than this one almanac.

If you're the type of person who uses tunnel vision to burrow deep into the minutest of topics until you know everything there is to know about it, this book is not for you. But if you're like me and prefer a more inclusive, superficial approach to life's obstacles and are willing to absorb minor injuries and major embarrassments in the pursuit of that lifestyle, *How to Do Everything* is your one-stop service manual.

Remember: true personal freedom comes from mind-numbing naïveté and a roll of duct tape.

Red Green

HOW TO SURVIVE THE SEVEN STAGES OF MARRIAGE: Denial, Guilt, Anger, Depression, The Upward Turn, Reconstruction, Acceptance

For a variety of reasons, human beings find it desirable to stay married to the same person for a long, long, long, long time. Sometimes it's love, sometimes it's convenience, sometimes it's just so the other person can't testify against them. Whatever the reason, staying married is not easy to do. In fact, for many people it's a source of grief. If that's how it is for you, try using the Seven Stages of Grief as guideposts on your journey towards marital bliss. Or at least as a way of controlling your homicidal urges.

1. Denial

This initial stage usually manifests itself shortly after the wedding. There are many symptoms, but the common thread is that you're continuing the same behaviour you enjoyed prior to getting married—hanging out with your single friends, coming home late without phoning, trying to meet women on the Internet, etc. These habits are inappropriate now that you are a husband. You must get through the denial stage quickly, or it could outlast the marriage.

2. Guilt

After the first year of marriage, you will start hearing a small voice in the back of your head, making you feel guilty about your unacceptable levels of grooming, your inappropriate responses in social situations and your insensitivity towards your spouse.

This small voice will be very familiar to you because it is your wife's. When it becomes your own voice doing the behaviour modification, you will have successfully passed through the guilt stage and will be ready to meet the next challenge.

3. Anger

The day will come (usually right after an argument you lost) when you start to feel a sense of resentment towards the institution of marriage. You'll be focused on the loss of personal freedom and the need for permission in every aspect of your existence. This resentment will turn to anger as you contemplate how your life could have been if you had never married. Instead of a home, you could own a Corvette. Instead of having a stressful corporate position, you could be a surfer. Instead of being a respected and responsible member of your community, you could be a boy toy in Monte Carlo. At the anger stage, it is helpful to talk with close friends (especially female ones) who can update you on your realistic options. It may be hard for you to hear, but if you are mature enough to accept their advice, you will be on track to returning to a happy marriage. Yes, I suppose the sight of you as a Corvette-driving surfer boy toy in Monte Carlo would be an entertaining one for the locals, but you're much better off in an environment where someone has already vowed to take responsibility for you.

4. Depression

After the anger dissipates, the next stage is a deep sadness from the realization that married life isn't as great as you expected and it's only going to get worse. This is the period when sleeping with your wife becomes exactly that. Conversations between you become short and fact-based. "It's garbage night." "Yeah, yeah." It's a period that's often marked by significant weight gain and an increase in the number of empty bottles in the recycling bin. Some couples have a brief trial separation, which may be as simple as one of them getting a job. But the key to getting through this stage is to realize that being depressed about the relationship you're in is actually more unpleasant than the relationship itself. When you see depression for what it is—nature's way of taking a bad situation and making it worse—you're ready to move on to the next stage.

5. The Upward Turn

The good side of depression is that it sinks you below reality, which means that as you come back to reality you're actually moving up. Now you have some upward momentum, and if you can find a way to sustain it, you're on your way to your version of a happy marriage. This is a very important stage, and you must be prepared to do everything in your power to maintain that upward movement. I recommend asking a police artist to do what they call "age progressions" on your photographs of old girlfriends. Seeing what they look like now will remove your sense of lost opportunities. Next, you need to spend time with some really miserable husbands and encourage them to tell you all of their horror stories. It'll be worth picking up the bar bill, because by the time they're finished, you'll feel like the luckiest man alive.

6. Reconstruction

This is your best opportunity to rebuild your marriage. You now have a much better sense of the structural weaknesses and the materials you're working with. You may not ever know what exactly your wife wants, but you have at least ten years of evidence of what she doesn't want. So start by not giving her any of that stuff. Start dressing better, lose a few pounds, put the seat down. She'll notice you stepping up your game and she'll step up hers. Even if you're not sure you still love your wife, pretend that you do, and pretty soon you will.

7. Acceptance

This is the final stage of marriage. This is the goal, the point where you acknowledge that, all in all, you got a very fair return on your investment and really have nothing major to complain about. As in almost all of the other stages, the best way to accomplish this goal is to put aside your biases and seek an accurate evaluation of yourself. I know it's impossible to stop you from being judgmental; instead, I'm asking to apply that attitude to you. For starters, go to the wax museum and get your picture taken standing beside the statue of Brad Pitt. Then show the picture around and see if anybody has difficulty picking out which one is you. Next, go on Google and find a list of the five hundred richest men in the world. Is your name on it? Stop ten strangers on the street and ask them if they know who you are. Okay, so now you have some sense of where you fit in the rich, famous or good-looking category. Next, draw a vertical line down the middle of a piece of paper. On one side, write the nice things your wife has done for you over the years. On the other side, write down the nice things you've done for her. If you run out of room on her side, there's probably available space on yours. These exercises will not only bring you to the level of acceptance needed to keep your marriage together, they will introduce the shared ingredient that's going to make the remaining years of marriage the best yet—gratitude.

DOCKING A POWERBOAT

The simplest way to dock a powerboat is to come in at a good speed towing a water skier. When you get close enough to the dock that you can hear the screaming from the onlookers, make a sharp turn and kill the engine. This will snap the water skier up onto the dock, from where they can pull your boat in backwards using the tow rope.

If the water-skier technique is no longer an option because everybody you know has finally wisened up, you're forced to use a more conventional approach. Powerboats are very difficult to steer at low speed, so make sure you're coming in at a fairly good clip. When you're within a few hundred yards, scan up and down the face of the dock, looking for something soft and spongy to aim at. Inflatable dinghies are ideal or, failing that, cedar strip canoes have a tendency to buckle, which allows them to absorb shock. The ability to absorb shock is really at the core of any docking attempt. In the absence of inflatables or canoes, sailboats are generally less expensive than powerboats, so pick one and go for it. And since it's a sailboat, there's a pretty good chance the owner won't be onboard—especially if he's married. For those of you who don't enjoy loud noises, harsh words or lawsuits, there is a kinder, gentler way to bring your powerboat in: go to the middle of the lake and shut the engine off. After a few minutes, observe which direction the wind and waves are making the boat drift—let's say it's southeast. To dock your boat, simply drive until the dock is southeast of you, kill the engine and let nature take its course. (Caution: If you have a small bladder, nature taking its course may not be a good thing.) While you're drifting in, it's a good idea to look around the lake for other docks, just in case the wind changes direction. This technique can take a long time, causing you to be late getting to your job. Which is a problem unless you're retired or work for the government.

HOW TO KEEP BIRDS AWAY

One of the great joys of suburban life is to be able to cook out on your back patio, wearing pants with an elastic waistband. But so often we hear horror stories of how birds are ruining that sacred life experience. Birds can be loud and annoying when they land on your picnic table or sit threateningly on the rim of your drink. Particularly offensive are the bird droppings that sometimes—like, say, on a pizza—are not all that easy to spot. So you want a solution that, ideally, will cause the birds to go else-where but at least, on the droppings issue, cause the birds to *go* elsewhere. Here's how simple that can be:

1) Get four large rectangular fans and mount each of them on four pieces of wood. Two of these legs should be long and two short, as shown. I suggest that for the pieces of wood, you saw up old rulers. That way you won't have to do any measuring.

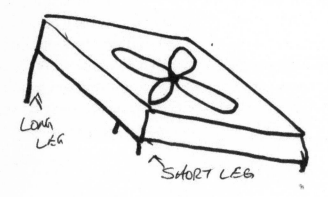

2) Lay the fans down so that the wooden supports create a gap for the air intake. Do not put the fans over grass, particularly if you own a dog. When positioning the fans, you must decide which of your neighbours you like least, then position the short legs so that the fans are slightly angled towards that neighbour's home.

3) Plug all four fans into one extension cord and have the power controlled by a motion detector that points straight up to the area above your patio.

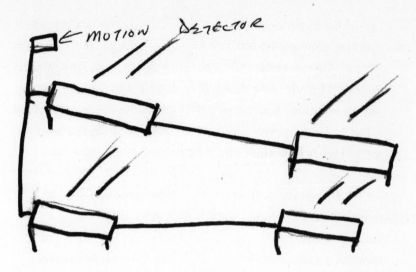

When a bird flies over, the motion detector will turn on the fans, which will provide a powerful upward thermal, making it virtually impossible for the bird to land on the patio. And if he decides to relieve himself as a sign of disapproval, the offending dropping will either be blown right back up the orifice from whence it came, or will be hurtled over the fence into your neighbour's pool.

After a few days of running this system, you will find that the birds stop coming over to your yard at all. Unfortunately, I can't say the same for your neighbour.

HOW TO DRINK RESPONSIBLY

The most dangerous aspect of alcohol consumption, other than the way it decreases your liver function and increases your flammability, is the debilitating effect it has on your decision-making skills. The truth is that your decision to have that first drink is the only truly sober one you will make that evening, and perhaps all weekend. That is because of alcohol's ability to block the body's natural instinct to say "No, thank you." Only someone who'd had nine drinks would think that a tenth was a good idea. Of course, the best solution is to just drink water—or, if water is too strong for you, you could try Michelob Ultra. Not drinking alcohol is always the best option, but, hey, let's be serious. I suggest you restrict yourself to beer. It has a lower alcohol content than wine or spirits and even has fewer calories per ounce than those other choices. And as an added bonus the diuretic component of beer means you'll be getting regular exercise. So the next time you go to a party, I suggest you take a case of beer. But before you leave the house, here's what you should do to help you make better decisions throughout the evening:

1) Take all twelve bottles out of the case and number the empty slots. At the party, make sure you drink the bottles in numerical order.

2) Get a small bottle of appliance paint and use the tiny brush to print notes at the bottom of some of the bottle slots (make sure the paint is white, even if your appliances are turquoise ones purchased in the late '60s).

3) In the first slot, print HAVE A GOOD TIME. It's a light-hearted, jovial message that will help put you in the party mood without massive injections of alcohol. Reinsert the beer bottle into the first slot.

4) In the second slot, print YOU MAY NOT BE JOHNNIE WALKER, BUT YOU ARE NOW A WALKER, JOHNNY as a clever and perhaps even witty reminder that you can no longer pass a Breathalyzer test. Reinsert the second and third bottles into their slots.

5) In the fourth slot, print YOU'RE NOT SMARTER OR FUNNIER THAN YOU WERE YESTERDAY, as a reminder that you're deluding yourself if you think four beers make you more interesting or entertaining to the other guests. Reinsert the fourth and fifth bottles into their slots.

6) In the sixth slot, print—in larger letters—STOP TALKING TO WOMEN. This will save you from embarrassment and/or

yelling, slapping and legal action. Reinsert the sixth bottle into its slot.

7) In the seventh slot, use even larger letters to print STOP TALKING TO EVERYBODY. It's time for a break—for *everybody*. Reinsert the seventh bottle into its slot.

8) In the eight, ninth and tenth slots, insert bottles of non-alcoholic beer. By this point, you won't notice. This will give you a chance to rejoin the party.

9) In the eleventh slot, in capitals, print LIE DOWN. When the time comes, try to have someone there who can explain that to you. Reinsert the eleventh bottle into its slot.

10) In the twelfth slot, print "911." Insert your cell phone into the slot. Ask the police to trace the call. That's your ride home—well, it's your ride *somewhere*.

THINGS NOT TO SAY TO THE BRIDE

We've all been there. The ceremony went as planned: the mother of the groom crying because she's losing her favourite son, the father of the bride crying because he's paying. The registry has been signed, the wedding pictures have all been taken, and now here you are in the reception line because your buddy Doug is the groom. In a few seconds you'll be face to face with the bride and you'll need to say something. Naturally, you'll do whatever you think is appropriate, but here are a few comments that have generally not been well received:

· How much did those shoes set you back?
· Well ... tonight's the night (wink).
· You're the only one of Doug's girlfriends that had any class.
· Is that dress white, or off-white?

9

- Do you know if the potatoes are real or instant?
- Tell Doug I cancelled the stripper.
- When you get a chance, I wouldn't mind a beer.
- I guess Doug's tests came back negative.
- Mind if I take a boo at the pre-nup?
- That veil really works for you.
- Jeez, I thought Doug was gay.

HOW TO BALANCE YOUR JOB AND HOME LIFE

One of the biggest problems ruining society today is that working people, especially men, become too focused on their careers and lose sight of the truly important things in life. Don't let that happen to you. Here are some warning signs that can indicate you have A.D.R.F.F.G.G.O. (Attention Deficit Regarding Family and Friends and General Goofing Off)

- You haven't taken a sick day this week and it's already Wednesday.
- You've had one or more promotions since starting with the company.
- When there's a problem at work, they call you.
- You have your own office.
- You have your own desk.
- You have your own parking spot.
- You have your own suit.
- When you're sleeping, you dream about work. Even when you're already AT work.
- If you add up the total number of hours in a year and find that you are spending in excess of 10 per cent of that time at your job, you may have an A.D.R.F.F.G.G.O. problem.

If you answered yes to any of the above, here are some steps you can take to reverse this dangerous trend before it's too late.

- Befriend unemployed people. That way, when you take a day off work, you have someone to hang with.
- Rationalize your attitude. Convince yourself that you're being paid half of what you're worth. Instead of killing yourself working hard for a raise you're probably never going to get, find ways to get out of working so that you're only being productive half the time. That's the same thing as getting twice the pay.
- Connect with your children by learning about their lives. While they're at school, stay home and play their video games.
- Initiate meaningful conversation with your wife by watching Oprah with her.
- Have a good reason not to go to work. Own only one suit and make sure it's at the cleaners most of the time.
- Join every religion so you qualify for all of their holidays.
- If by some fluke this behaviour leads to your termination, have a discussion with your wife, concluding with the realization that one of you is going to have to find gainful employment. Then it's just a matter of playing the waiting game with her. If you've been married for more than ten years, I'm guessing you're used to that.

HOW TO REDUCE YOUR HOTEL BILL

Let's say that, through no fault of your own, you end up staying at a nice hotel. Sure, it's great to have the movie channels and the Jacuzzi, but the free chocolates give you pimples and the terry-cloth bathrobes are too bulky to fit into your suitcase. So, all in all, it's just way too expensive. Here's what you do. Before you check out, a hotel guy will come into your room and take inventory of your mini-bar, and the results of that audit will be applied to your bill. If you take a look at the mini-bar prices, you'll see that a can of domestic beer is $8. So you go out immediately and buy a case of twenty-four cans of beer, bring them back to the room and stuff them into every available nook and cranny in your mini-bar. Now, when he does the audit, you will get a credit for twenty-four cans of beer at $8 each. That's $192. Suddenly, a $200 hotel room will only cost you eight bucks.

QUICK TIP #1: OPENING A PICKLE JAR

Banging the rim of the lid with the back of a knife or running hot water over the jar may not be options if you are behind in your electric bill and are not allowed to have sharp objects. So instead, hammer a cold chisel down through the centre of the lid and wedge it in there, attach Vise-Grips to the chisel and use them to unscrew the lid. The jar will no longer be airtight, but that will make your fridge smell better. And after you've eaten all the pickles, you have a dandy piggy bank.

PLUMBING MADE EASY

For the beginner handyman, plumbing is one of the few non-life-threatening do-it-yourself activities. The worst that can happen is that at the end of it you will either be all wet or covered with sewage—just another day at the office. So here are a few simple tips that can help you learn from the mistakes of others.

- Water runs downhill, so before you start any project put a high-volume pump at the lowest spot in your basement and make sure it has a float switch so it turns on automatically. Run a large output hose from the pump through the nearest basement window and aim it at the neighbour's house that is lower than yours. Now you're ready to start plumbing.
- ~~Step One: Turn off the water.~~ Step One: Make sure your wife has finished using the bathroom, then turn off the water.
- Drain the system by turning on all the taps, flushing all the toilets, opening the drain on the hot water heater and drinking cocktails until the fridge ice-maker is empty.
- Most supply-side plumbing uses copper pipe, which can be soldered easily. If you have galvanized steel pipe in your house, you probably have lead deposits in your brain and should not be operating a propane torch.
- Clean and lightly sand all pipe ends and fittings—and while you're at it, give yourself a manicure.
- Apply flux to the cleaned joints. (CAUTION: Flux is a difficult word to say and should be pronounced carefully when asking your wife where it is.)
- Heat the joint with a propane torch until the solder melts and flows into it. If you're soldering over your head, start by spraying your face with Pam. Keep adding

solder until it flows evenly around the entire joint. Don't use too much; there have been cases of excess solder pouring from the joint and fusing the plumber's steel-toed boot to the bathtub drain. Don't let that happen to you.

- Allow the joint to cool. If you can place the palm of your hand on the joint without screaming, it's cool enough. Before you turn the water back on, wrap the joint you fixed, and anything else that you touched, with duct tape. Professional plumbers know that duct tape only works on dry pipes.

- Referring back to the concept of water flowing downhill, you'll want to be standing much higher than the joint you fixed while you turn the water back on. This may require a complex series of belts, chains, pulleys and sprockets, particularly if you fixed the attic toilet and the main water valve is in the basement. Another option is to send your son down to turn the water on.

- When you turn the water on, you may hear hissing or spraying sounds. That's because you forgot to turn all the taps off after you drained the system. What an idiot.

- I hope it all works out great, but if it doesn't, you can always yell for more flux.

HOW TO FORM A CLUB

There is a randomness to life that brings with it a stream of unexpected situations and occurrences that many people find annoying. One of the antidotes to this is to form a club—a group of people of similar interests who get together regularly to do the same things. It's a way of knowing that, on the first

Wednesday of every month, you'll be getting together with a bunch of guys you sort of like, doing something you more or less enjoy. Now, I know there are a bunch of clubs already in existence, but they may have members that you wouldn't get along with, so you're better off to start your own club and thereby have complete control over who gets in. You may be accused of being biased or discriminatory, but your best defence is that all clubs are based on the premise of keeping people out. There is only one club that includes everybody—it's called the human race, the dues are high and they rarely have meetings. So I suggest you form a new club that nobody has done before. Something that's exciting and fun and gives people a chance to express their individuality while in a group setting.

I suggest you start an oil change club. It's easy: all you need is a minimum of four guys with cars, two forty-foot steel I-beams, three 45-gallon drums, a length of eavestrough, a large package of Tensor bandages and a liability waiver. You can meet once a month at the top of a hill (in case there's spillage) and make it BYOW (bring your own wrench). You could also get logo T-shirts and hats and leather jackets with a big oil can embossed on the back, but I suggest you start small. You will need a name for your oil change club—the City Slickers or the Slippery Slopes or the Crude Dudes or the Oily Birds. Or, my personal favourite, the Oil Change Club. And the benefits of having an oil change club are tremendous. You get to hang with guys who like to change their own oil—a dying breed. Plus you'll be able to buy in bulk, so you'll save money on oil, rags and who knows what all. And other things that are also good.

Before the first meeting, you need each guy to know how heavy his car is. You can do this by pulling into a truck weigh station on the highway and claiming, "I thought this was a McDonald's, but while I'm here, how much does my car weigh?" At the meeting, after you've done the opening ceremonies and sung the anthem and done the secret handshake, have the guys line their cars up in order of weight, from the lightest to the heaviest, then drive them up to the I-beams you've arranged as seen in the diagram.

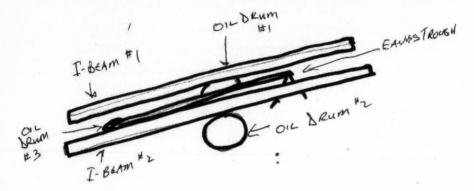

(You can purchase I-beams very cheaply now that almost all of the factories in North America are being closed and torn down. eBay has the lowest prices, but they really zing you on the shipping charges.) Run the piece of eavestrough up the centre of the I-beam set-up. Have the eavestrough on a slight downward slope so that anything that falls into it will run into the forty-five-gallon drum buried at the far end.

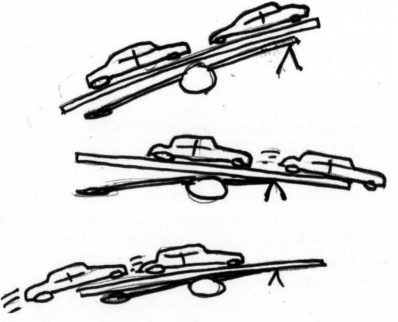

Drive the first two cars onto the I-beams as pictured. The second car is heavier, so that will keep the first car elevated. Drain the oil from that car and replace the plug. Probably not a good idea to run the car without any oil in the engine, so put the first car in neutral and use the second car to push it towards the end of the I-beam until you reach the tipping point, as shown in the diagram. The I-beam will swing down, allowing the first car to roll off to the filling area, where it can be filled with new oil and driven out of the way. When the first car rolls off the I-beam, the balance will shift and the I-beam will return to its normal position. Now, drive the third car onto the I-beam and move the second car forward as shown in the diagram. Drain the oil from the second car and repeat the process for as many cars and members as you have in your club.

Now, I know that cost savings and responsible attention to auto maintenance are obvious pluses of the whole oil change club phenomenon, but there's so much more: the camaraderie, the brotherhood, the good times, the hilarity of watching grown men with oily hands trying to pick up tools or drive their cars, the love and trust that grow out of close friends staying long after dark to help you find your drain plug. These are memories that last a lifetime. Or three thousand miles.

HOME SCHOOLING

Everyone in this country has the right to home-school their children. And while it means your children will be home with you seven days a week, fifty-two weeks a year, there are several benefits. So before you automatically dismiss the concept as unworkable or somehow beneath you, take a look at all of the pros and cons:

PRO:
- You know he's actually attending school.

CON:
- You can't get away from him.

PRO:
- Suddenly school has flex-hours.
- Parent-Teacher Night is a love-in.
- Your child doesn't get exposed to other opinions.

CON:
- Your child doesn't get exposed to other opinions.

PRO:
- He's never going to know more than you.

CON:
- He's never going to know more than you.

PRO:
- He has a very good chance of passing.
- No need to buy teacher a fridge magnet as a Christmas present.
- He won't have to get on a bus.
- He can take thirty-seven years to complete high school.

CON:
- He can take thirty-seven years to complete high school.

PRO:
- You can see what he is eating and drinking.
- You will have a much more complete picture of what your child is like.

CON:

- He can see what you're eating and drinking.
- He will have a much more complete picture of what you're like.

REVIVING TRADITIONS OF THE PAST

I came across some good news in the barbershop the other day, and for a guy my age there's hardly ever good news in a barbershop. I have so much hair loss I should be getting my haircuts for free, but the barber says it costs more than ever because he adds a finder's fee.

So while I waited for him to take a little off the side and a little more off the wallet, I started reading a magazine article about Europe in the early 1900s. Most of the homes in Europe are hundreds of years old because they were built before things like insulbrick or vinyl siding or real estate developers. But houses that old need a lot of maintenance to keep them looking fresh. So back then, if you saw a house that needed a coat of paint or some chimney repointing, you knew that the owners were short of money. If the house was looking just fine, you knew the owners were getting by. But if the house was completely falling apart—get this—it meant the owners were incredibly rich. It was called "benign neglect." Something to do with old money or another way of telling the neighbours, "Our family is so powerful that we can ignore the forces of nature and be just fine." It's the same logic that led to inbreeding.

But I'm thinking we need to bring that whole benign neglect thing back. Suddenly, my home and garden will look like they belong to the Sultan of Brunei. The missing shingles, the cracked windows, the charred tree beside the barbecue—all signs that this guy has deep pockets. And why stop at property? Benign neglect would also work well as a fitness regime. The worse shape you're in, the richer you look, because the coded message is, "Whatever part of my body blows up, I have enough money to get it fixed or replaced."

USE THIS, NOT THIS

The expression "Use the right tool for the job" has become a cliché for everyone from politicians to artificial inseminators, but it remains truer than ever among the handymen who originated it. When there's a specific repair or renovation job to be done and there's a choice to be made between (a) finesse and (b) expediency, a disturbing number of handymen answer "never" to (a) and "always" to (b). As a way to reverse that trend, here's a handy guide to help you use the right tool for the job:

JOB	USE THIS	NOT THIS
Jewellery Repair	Needle-Nosed Pliers	Pipe Wrench
Toilet Removal	Channellock Wrench	Nitroglycerine
Car Dent Removal	Rubber Mallet	Bowling Ball
Removing Wallpaper	Scraper	Thumbnail
Refinishing Antiques	Paint Stripper	Propane Torch
Tree Stump Removal	Bush Hog	Nitroglycerine
Cutting Rebar	Bench Vice	Your Knees
Replacing Circuit Board	Soldering Iron	Arc Welder
Removing Steering Wheel	Hub Puller	Crowbar
Replacing Roof Shingles	Extension Ladder	Fruit Tree
Fitting Crown Moulding	Mitre Box	Chainsaw
Male Pattern Baldness	Good Haircut	Bad Toupee
Halitosis	Oral Hygiene	Chewing Tobacco
Dispute with Neighbour	Hand of Friendship	Nitroglycerine

HOW TO APOLOGIZE

Of all the skills a person can learn in their lives, none is more important than the art of the apology. There are just so many situations in life where nothing but an apology will do. And yet it's a complex and mystifying science, because there are so many variables creating so many different dynamics in so many situations that it's not always easy to know what the correct apology should be. And giving the *wrong* apology is worse than no apology at all. Here's what you need to know.

APOLOGY #1 — When you're expected to apologize even though you have nothing to apologize for.

This doesn't happen nearly as often as you think it does. So if you've made a habit out of underestimating your own guilt, you are probably also good at underestimating the other person's intelligence. This attitude will lead you to making a half-hearted, sarcastic apology that will do more harm than good. That's because of the cardinal rule of apologies: the less obliged you feel to give an apology, the more sincere that apology must be. The best solution is a simple, straightforward "I screwed up. I'm sorry." Don't qualify your apology by adding "but what the hell were you thinking?" In fact, any sentence with the word *but* in it is not an apology. If you put a *but* in your apology, somebody's liable to kick it.

APOLOGY #2 — When you're afraid that an apology will be like pleading guilty.

This is a tricky one. Maybe you were sleeping on some shelving in a corner of the warehouse when you got a severe leg cramp and kicked over the small electric heater you had in there with you, which led to a serious of unfortunate coincidences involving a large propane tank and the eventual blowing off of the factory roof. Nobody really has any idea of what happened, and you feel bad about it, but you're afraid an apology may cost you your job.

The best solution is to tell your boss you're sorry, but don't get specific—just that you're sorry that crazy things like this just happen, and if there's anything you can do, like take a cut in pay or help pay for a new roof, you'd be happy to do that. Chances are he won't suspect a thing. If he hired you in the first place, he's obviously not that hard to fool.

APOLOGY #3 — When an apology isn't enough.

This is the big daddy of apologies. You know you have to apologize, but your mistake was so huge that an apology alone is not going to cut it. The danger here is that the apology becomes the thin edge of the wedge leading to a lifetime of attempted restitution in an effort to get the scales of justice back to even. That's why the quid pro quo has to be part of the apology. "I'm sorry. I was wrong. I feel badly about it, and to make it up to you, I will buy you another cow." That way, when they accept your apology, they're also accepting the terms under which your relationship can get back to what it was.

APOLOGY #4 — When you think the apology should be going the other way.

We've all had situations where things were said and done by both parties, and now you're expected to apologize when in fact you feel the other person should be apologizing to you. This requires finesse and subtlety. You need to adjust your thinking a little. You need to accept that you are partially to blame, even if you're not. Stubbornness is your enemy here. But that doesn't mean you're the only one to blame, and your apology can reflect that position. "I know some hurtful things have been said and done on both sides, and I for one feel badly about my part in that and feel I owe you an apology." Now, wait a few seconds for their response (i.e., apology). If it's not forthcoming, you are justified to add, "So, do you accept my apology?" They'll answer yes, and then you say, "Me too." And leave the room immediately.

HOW TO GET A JOB

There may be times in your adult life when you are unemployed, occasionally through no fault of your own. But regardless of how you got yourself into that predicament, the only way out is to find yourself other employment. And to do that, you will probably need to have a successful job interview. Here's how:

Overdress. Show respect for the job by dressing a few levels above what you'll be wearing if you get it. If you'll be wearing coveralls, wear a suit. If you'll be wearing a suit, wear a tuxedo. If you'll be wearing a paper hat, wear a felt fedora. Give the impression that you are just slightly overqualified. Generally, the interviewer will put more stock in how you look than in what you say. Good thing.

Drop the bravado. Pretending you don't need the job makes you look like an idiot. If you didn't want the job, you wouldn't be at the interview. So instead of focusing on the contempt you have for the position that's being offered, try to present yourself as the best possible candidate, even though we all know it's a crappy job.

Do a little grooming. Get your hair washed and cut. If you don't have hair, get a buff. Don't wear any body ornaments that indicate an attitude—earring, nose ring, lip ring, nipple ring, mood ring. Cover up your tattoos, even if it means wearing a long-sleeved turtleneck sweater and a Tensor bandage around your forehead.

Keep your answers short. The less you say, the better. Give pointed responses that directly answer the question. Don't assume that the interviewer knows everything about you. Most criminal records are kept confidential.

Stay positive. Try to say yes a lot during the interview. It's what you want *them* to eventually say, so it's good to set that trend. If your attitude is negative, they may reject you just to give you another thing to complain about.

Act like you already have the job. If it's a maintenance position, walk in with a wet plunger and tell the guy that you fixed the men's room toilet on the way in. He'll be impressed, even if he won't shake hands.

Don't dwell in the past. Try to steer all of the questions towards the future—how you're going to handle this new job, rather than how you mishandled the last six. If the interviewer keeps referring to difficulties you've had at previous jobs, make that an asset by pointing out that only somebody who'd gone through those problems would have learned from those mistakes. Focus on the worst mistake you've ever made and remind them that the charge was reduced to manslaughter.

Stay in the moment. This interview is not really about how you're going to perform in the job once you get it. Nobody really cares about that. It can't be too important a job if they're interviewing *you* for it. They just don't want to hire anybody who's really going to screw things up. As long as you're prepared to do an average job, everybody will be happy enough. What really matters is the interviewer's perception right now, at this moment. You may not be enjoying the interview process, but think of how they must feel about it. They have to interview thirty or forty candidates, most of whom are like you. They want the process to be over too. So just tell them exactly what they want to hear—that you're capable, you're available and you have enough pride to do the job at a satisfactory level, but not enough to ever be looking for any kind of promotion. Chances are they'll hire you because they feel the same way about their job.

HOW TO TELL IF YOU HAVE A PROBLEM TEENAGER

- The other kids come home in an orange school bus with flashing red lights. Your son comes home in a black-and-white car with flashing blue lights.
- On Parent-Teacher Night, the teacher is unaware that your son is enrolled.
- All of the mail your son receives comes in the form of registered letters.
- He says he entered a contest and won a trip to Colombia.
- There's always a bright light burning in the attic and your electricity bill is five thousand dollars a month.
- His friends are a lot older than him, and he can only visit them on Sundays between 2 and 4 P.M.
- He brought the family car home with no gas in the tank because it leaked out through the bullet holes.
- He gave you his class picture. There was a front-on shot and a profile.
- You were doing the laundry and found a knife in his sock.
- He has a court-appointed lawyer on speed dial.
- His friends have rodent nicknames.
- During dinner conversations, he pleads the Fifth.
- He receives cards on Father's Day.

QUICK TIP #2: WHAT TO DO ABOUT SQUEAKY FLOOR-BOARDS

Identify the section of the floor where the floorboards squeak. Remove the board in the middle of the section. Insert an inflated whoopee cushion and lay the board back down on top of it. In a couple of days the whole family will walk lightly on the floor or go around it completely, and the annoying squeak will be a thing of the past.

BAD GIFT WEATHER STATION

One of the great assets in adapting to your environment is the ability to make the best of a bad situation, as many people discover when they try Internet dating. Over the course of your life you've probably received some really bad gifts that are either lying in a drawer somewhere or being used to shim up one of the dining-room table legs. It would be so much better if you could turn them into useful, productive items.

The main problem with bad gifts is that they bear no connection to your interests or needs. They are a supply for which there is no demand. As soon as you redeploy them into an area you're interested in, they become the greatest gifts ever. (I may have overshot a little there.) So, what are men most interested in? Well, next to the obvious, it's the weather. So here's how you can turn a few dumb, useless gifts into a state-of-the-art backyard weather station.

MEN'S SUIT RACK

This thing is supposed to stand at the end of the bed, holding your suit, shirt, tie and pants neatly for you to wear to work the next morning. Talk about useless. If you have a suit and a job, chances are you also have a closet. All this does is give you something to trip over in the night or scare the wits out of you when you wake up and think a well-dressed leprechaun is staring at you. The suit rack works much better as the stand for your new weather station.

MOOSE THERMOMETER

This is a huge thermometer with a picture of a moose on it. It's about two feet in diameter and doesn't go with any of your home décor, with the possible exception of the inside of the chimney. This

is a gift with what's called proximity sensitivity—the closer you are to it, the less you like it. So put it on the suit rack, out in the middle of the backyard. If possible, accentuate the colour of the temperature indicator so that from a distance you see more needle and less moose.

HULA GIRL TIE

Ties like this, with a hula girl or something like that on them, are seen by the world as a great big "Hello, I have a drinking problem." It will have a far less negative impact on your image when used as a wind-speed indicator on your suit-rack weather station. In time, you will be able to calibrate the body parts and severity of the hula girl's gyrations to actual wind speeds. If you want to take it up another notch, attach the tie to the knob on top of the suit rack with a loose Windsor knot, and it will be able to swing around freely to indicate wind direction as well as speed.

SINGING FISH

I know you probably really loved this when you first got it and turned it on to watch the mouth, head and fin movements while it sang "Proud Mary." But ten minutes later, it got old. So now what? Well, how about using it as the indicator portion of your precipitation meter? In lay terms, that means the fish will start singing when it rains. But you need to also hook up a triggering mechanism. See below.

HAIR-RESTORER PILLS

I sincerely hope you bought these for yourself, because from anyone else, it's cruel. From you, it's just stupid. If you come from a long line of bald men and you weren't adopted, chances are there's

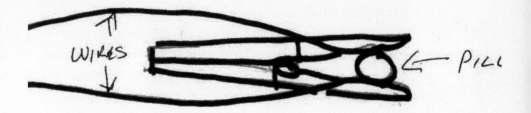

WIRES ← PILL

nothing in a jar that's going to overpower your genetic predisposition. But the pills still have value. They are going to be the triggering device for your precipitation meter. Remove the bare wires around the fish's on/off switch and mount them inside the jaws of a clothes peg, as shown. Now keep the jaws apart with one of the hair-restoring pills and mount the clothes peg at the top of the suit rack. When it rains, the pill will dissolve, the clothes peg will close, bringing the wires together, which will make the fish sing. Voila.

WHOOPEE-CUSHION BAROMETER

WHOOPEE!!

There is nothing funnier to an eleven-year-old boy than a whoopee cushion. Unfortunately, very few eleven-year-old boys are seen as world leaders or business tycoons or even heads of households. So a grown man with a whoopee cushion, unless he's Leslie Nielsen, is not anything anyone wants. Instead, use it as a barometer.

To set it initially, you have to go to the beach so that you're at sea level, and blow it up there. I suggest you go at night, because inflating a whoopee cushion on a busy beach can attract some unwanted attention from muscular lifeguards. Once you have it inflated, you can return home and mount the cushion anywhere on your suit rack. You will be able to tell if the air pressure is dropping because the whoopee cushion will get larger. You'll be able to *hear* if the pressure is rising, because the whoopee cushion will be compressed and will release its universal signal that there's too much pressure somewhere. Prolonged periods of high pressure will necessitate another trip to the beach.

PUTTING IT ALL TOGETHER

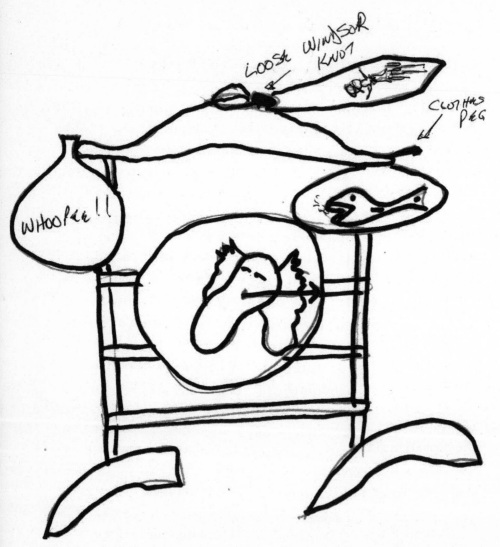

You wake up in the morning to the chorus of "Proud Mary" coming from a rubber fish. It must be raining. You look out the window to see the hula girl dancing from the northwest at sixty gyrations an hour. The temperature is past the moose's antlers, so it's a warm enough day. If only the air pressure would rise, that would mean better weather is on its way. And then you hear the sound of good news coming from the whoopee cushion. Or at least you sincerely *hope* that's what you just heard.

HOW TO CHECK YOUR MARITAL STATUS

Often when you fill out an application form, there's a space where they ask you your marital status. That's not what I'm talking about here. If you don't know whether you're married or single, you are living either with dementia or in Hollywood. I'm talking about marital status in the sense of how your wife is feeling about you at any particular moment. It's important for a man to always know exactly where he stands, as his marital status will affect his ability to enjoy the pleasures of life, liberty and the pursuit of happiness. It is also a cruel twist of fate that a man can unwittingly get himself into a lot of trouble with his significant other, and the "unwittingly" part only exacerbates the problem. So the best approach for any man is to find subtle ways to evaluate the current situation and then work backwards to find the origin of the problem so that he can begin to make restitution.

SECTION A

The process begins when you enter the front door and announce your arrival. How does your wife respond?

> *Worst Response:* No response. You'd better hope she's not home. Score 0 points.
>
> *Second-Worst Response:* A muffled greeting from a distant room—could mean minor trouble. Score 5 points.
>
> *Better Response:* She comes to the door to greet you with a hug and a kiss. Score 10 points.

Best Response: She comes to the door to greet you with a beer and a snack and the bed's not made. Score, and get 15 points.

The next step is to casually assess how your wife is dressed and groomed and pay attention to the non-verbal sounds she makes.

Worst Response: She's still in her pajamas and robe and hasn't combed her hair or put on any make-up. She sighs all the time and keeps trying to lie down. Score 0 points.

Second-Worst Response: She's dressed in business attire, has her hair in a tight bun, her brow is permanently furrowed, and she clears her throat while she looks right through you. Score 5 points.

Better Response: She's nicely dressed with a soft, clean hairstyle and she's humming Broadway musicals. Score 10 points.

Best Response: She's wearing *your* pajamas, sighs all the time and keeps trying to lie down. Score 15 points.

Move on to asking her about what she would like to do about dinner.

Worst Response: "I'm going out with friends. Your dinner is in the doggie dish." Score 0 points.

Second-Worst Response: "Let's get cleaned up and go to an expensive restaurant." Score 5 points.

Better Response: "I have a coupon for the drive-thru." Score 10 points.

Best Response: "I'll make fries while you barbecue the steaks. Than I'll set up the TV trays while you grab the remote." Score 15 points.

And now the ultimate test: trying to have a conversation. There's so much you can learn from her behaviour.

Worst Response: She stares at you for a long moment, lets out a long sigh and then leaves the room. Score 0 points.

Second-Worst Response: There is much too long a pause before she says anything. And she immediately goes off topic, bringing up something stupid you did twenty years ago. Score 5 points.

Better Response: Her pauses are way too short. She often speaks over the last half of your sentences. She's annoyed, but at least engaged. Score 10 points.

Best Response: She answers your questions and offers informed, logical suggestions to make both of your lives better. Score 15 points.

If you add up your score and it's less than 25 points, please proceed to Section B.

SECTION B

This is the time for complete honesty—you have screwed up, your wife is not happy and you have no idea what you did wrong or how to make it right. These two things are obviously connected, because if you knew what you did wrong, you'd be able to figure out what to do to correct it. And the worst part is you've let the problem go so long that now your wife is not the least bit interested in helping you identify it. So you must solve it totally on your own. Your women friends are on her side and are not going to help you. And your men friends are just as stupid as you are. So go to a quiet place where you can sit and think.

Cast your mind back in time to the last moment you can think of when your wife was happy. If you're going back more than a year, this is probably not going to accomplish anything. But let's say it was three weeks ago and you were on your way to a house party and your wife was in a really good mood as she was getting ready to go. Now concentrate and put yourself back there in that moment when she was happy, then play the scene forward from there—in slo-mo so you don't miss any detail. Try to focus on your memory of your wife's reaction to everything that was said and done from that moment on. (This exercise would have been a lot easier if you had paid attention at the time, but I know that's out of the question.)

Okay, so your wife's all ready, and before you leave she asks, "How do I look?" Try to remember your response. Was it perhaps somewhat critical or insincere? Did you sense a mood change in her? Did the furnace kick on?

Maybe you behaved inappropriately at the party or said something complimentary about someone else's wife or did that party piece thing that your wife has asked you a million times not to do. Whatever it is, if you slowly trace all the events, moving slowly forward, and try to reconstruct your wife's reaction to each of them, you will eventually stumble across the pivotal faux pas that placed you in the hell in which you are now residing. As soon as you identify that event, you must go to your wife and tell her that something is bothering you. It was this thing you did at the Johnsons' party with the grass skirt and the Jell-O, and it was a stupid thing to do and, more importantly, you are afraid that it embarrassed her and made her think that you don't love her, and nothing could be further from the truth. My guess is that even if you haven't identified the exact problem, you'll be close enough.

HOW TO PRESERVE YOUR INTERNAL HERMIT

Deep in the heart of every man is the urge to be a hermit. Even the Pope probably has days when he's looking for a little "me" time. Of course, very few of us can act on this urge, but repressing it can lead to anger and resentment. So the best solution is to have brief moments of the hermetic lifestyle, to recharge your batteries, and then you're ready to get back to being the loving husband and father and hale fellow well met that everybody has bought into all these years. So here are a few good-natured ways to grab that little respite of privacy and serenity that we all so desperately need.

•

- Put a DO NOT DISTURB sign on your ball cap.
- Spin the couch 180 degrees and slide it up to a bare wall, creating a hiding place/crib.
- Wear earphones all the time—with the other end plugged into your wallet.
- Redo your garage doors so they lock from the inside.
- Tell your wife you'll be in the basement for a while trying to get rid of a nest of mice. She'll let you stay down there as long as you want.
- Take up ice fishing.
- Set up your phone so that all of your incoming calls are forwarded to a telemarketing company.
- Wire your doorbell so that, instead of ringing, it sends a small electrical charge through the person's finger.
- Don't make eye contact with anyone, including yourself— unless you're cross-eyed, in which case you can't help it.
- Turn your welcome mat over and leave a few spent shotgun shells lying on the ground.
- Stay inside the house. If you absolutely must go out for something, take your shirt off to eliminate small talk.
- Put a QUARANTINED sign on your door. Make sure you spell it correctly—GUARANTEED is a different word.
- Get something odd smelling from a local farm and put a small pile of it in the bushes near your house.
- Put a NO HABLA INGLES sign on your door. If you live in Canada, make sure you also have it in French.
- Leave your garbage can at the end of the driveway with a hazardous waste sticker on it and a handful of glow-in-the-dark golf balls inside.
- If all of the above fails, just say what you think. To everybody. You'll be alone in no time.

INCOME TAX DEDUCTIONS THAT ARE WORTH A TRY

The quickest, easiest way to increase your income is by paying less tax. Even at the lowest income levels, if you can avoid income tax, that's like getting a 35-per-cent pay increase. I think we all know that there is nothing in your ability or work ethic that's going to see that happen any other way. So here are a few techniques that might be worth a try. Pick and choose the ones that suit your situation. Don't try them all unless you like prison food.

- All year, you buy beer at $30 a case and return the empties at $2.40. That's a tax-deductible investment loss of $27.60 times the number of cases you buy. You may need to use a calculator.
- The cost of gas and parking on your weekly visits to the unemployment office are a deductible business expense.
- If you make fries at a fast-food restaurant, your haircuts are a work-related safety measure and are therefore deductible.
- Striptease artists are allowed to deduct the cost of cough and cold medicines.
- Change your perspective. Instead of describing yourself as an unemployed, unskilled labourer who spends all day watching TV in his underwear, go with self-employed freelance video entertainment analyst. That makes deductions out of the TV, the cable bill, the snacks, even the underwear.
- Be an entrepreneur. If you know somebody who makes a good living—say, $100,000 a year—offer to help him pay less tax. He's probably in the 45-per-cent tax bracket, whereas you average in around the zero-per-cent mark. So, offer to split his income 50/50. That way, you each show a $50,000 income, on which you have

to each pay 35 per cent in income tax. You keep half of the tax savings as your fee. Without you, he'd pay $45,000 in tax and end up with $55,000 net. This way, you each pay 35 per cent of $50,000, which is $17,500, leaving each of you a net amount of $32,500. You then give him back $27,500 out of the $50,000 he originally gave you. He ends up with $60,000 net and you end up with $5,000 net. Everybody wins.

- The income-splitting approach is great for anyone who had a year without income, but if you have never been gainfully employed in your life, you have an opportunity to take it to a whole other level. That's because you can declare yourself an adult dependent and can then be claimed as a deduction by a high-income taxpayer. The best way to do this is to put yourself on eBay. A brief description of your lack of marketable abilities and your long, unblemished unemployment record will probably get better response if you don't include a picture. Once you start getting bids, you can negotiate whatever you want for the tax advantage you're getting. Cash could create a problem, since that would give you income and void your dependency status, which was the only thing you had going for you. Instead, you can either move to their city and live with them, or they can provide lodging for you in your own town. My guess is they'll go with Plan B.

- If you do, in fact, have the desire and capability to generate income, make sure you're self-employed and get paid in goods and services rather than in cash. If you fix somebody's truck, you get to use the truck for a month. If you build somebody a house, let them pay you in lumber. Or light fixtures. Or groceries. Anything but cash. If the government claims you need to send in 30 per cent of your income, mail them a few gallons of ice cream.

- A long time ago, income tax was introduced by the government as a temporary wartime measure. So when they come after you, just tell them you've decided not to pay income tax as a temporary PEACETIME measure. I find that, as a general rule, tax collectors have a very playful sense of humour.

BEHAVIOUR MODIFICATION THROUGH OBSERVATION

If you're not lucky enough to have a significant other constantly correcting your behaviour in social situations, there are ways that you can do it for yourself. You simply have to heighten your awareness and know what you're looking for. It's really just a matter of closely evaluating an environment as you enter it, then monitoring any changes resulting from your presence.

For example, when you enter a reception, you should notice the percentage of people who are more or less facing you as they stand and chat with each other. If that number decreases to zero per cent over the first thirty minutes, that's not a good sign. And if that number increases to 100 per cent, that can be an even worse sign, depending on how you're getting their attention.

Before you even enter the room, you should hover casually around the entrance and compare your appearance to that of the other attendees. Are you going to stand out in that orange velour jogging suit? Compare your hair to theirs. Is theirs combed? The objective is to fit in. You have to look like one of them to be one of them. If you pass that test, it's okay for you to go in, but do it slowly and make sure your senses are turned on. If you feel a subtle cool breeze in a private region, casually turn towards the corner and do up your fly.

People generally tend to get a drink right away, but this is a mistake. You should first take a close look at the hors d'oeuvres. If they're dry, fine. But if they're gooey or slippery and not the same colour as your shirt, that's just trouble waiting to happen. The cardinal rule of reception schmoozing is that gooey stuff cannot be eaten with one hand. So you need to either do all your hors d'oeuvres eating prior to getting a drink, or skip them and go straight to the booze. To get the most value, I recommend option one—eating first. Generally, an ounce of shrimp is worth more than an ounce of reception wine.

Now you're ready to engage in conversation. Here again, you need to pay attention to what's happening. If you're planning to spend a couple of hours at this event, you're much better off to get into a few longer conversations than to try taking on a whole bunch of mindless brief encounters. If you want to have a long conversation with someone, the sad truth is that at least half of the time you'll need to be doing the listening. If, in the first five minutes, you've been talking for at least four minutes, that conversation will soon come to an abrupt end. Pay attention to the other person's speech pattern. If they ask you a ten-second question, unless they're Barbara Walters they're not expecting anything more than a ten-second answer. Whenever possible, answer their question with a question of your own. That will give them a chance to participate in the conversation and will send out the message, true or false, that you have some interest in what they think. Tempo is another important factor. Wait until they've made their point, take a beat to think about it, then respond. Talking immediately after they stop, or talking over their last few words, sends out the message that you have all the answers—you need to keep that as your little secret. But the single most important conversational tool is to make sure you have a lot of eye contact with the person. That's the best way to tell if you are truly engaging them in a meaningful conversation. If you don't have much experience making eye contact, go to a pirates' convention and practise. Most of them only have one eye, so it's a lot easier.

HOW TO IMPROVE YOUR GAS MILEAGE ON A LONG TRIP

- Don't go.
- Failing that, go in someone else's car.
- Weight has a negative effect on fuel economy. Insist that fat passengers will not be allowed to ride in the car but will instead be sitting on lawn chairs in a flatbed trailer. (Tip: Get them to sign a waiver and only travel at night.)
- Don't have a specific departure date. When the wind is coming from behind you, that's the time to leave (a rule you may already live by).
- But seriously, wind resistance is an important factor. Remove anything that sticks out on your car—mirrors, loose fenders, the "up yours" finger on your radio antenna. If your hood has a habit of flying open at highway speed, remove it and leave it in the garage. When questioned by the police, tell them it's a safety measure that allows you to spot engine fires before they get dangerous.
- Anything that takes power from the engine, makes you burn more gas. Disconnect the air conditioning—if this makes any of your passengers smell funny, make them ride with the fat people in the trailer. Also, disconnect the power steering—you won't be turning that much on the highway, and manual steering will give you an excuse not to pull over to shop for antiques. Disconnect the vacuum assist for the power brakes—this will make the car a lot harder to stop, but when you find yourself speeding towards the edge of a cliff or a flaming bus, you'll be amazed at what adrenaline will allow you to do.
- Hills burn gas. Try to minimize them by making sure that a large portion of your trip is always through Saskatchewan.

- overinflate your tires. The goal is to get the tires so round they're barely touching the road. Also, try to hit potholes at maximum speed—airborne cars get excellent gas mileage.
- Get into the habit of turning your car off whenever you're at a red light or coasting down a hill or when a song that you don't like comes on the radio.
- If someone is tailgating you, slow down, but do it in such a casual, subtle way that the other driver doesn't notice. If you do it right, he won't feel the slight bump when the two cars touch, at which point you shift into neutral and let him push you. Sit back, enjoy the free ride and just ignore his horn.
- Rationalize. Let's say you're driving a car the size of a whale with an engine like a furnace and you're getting ten miles per gallon, while your politically correct neighbour drives an oversized football helmet with a model airplane engine that gets sixty mpg. Just change your perspective. His car is a two-seater at most, so on a gallon of gas he's moving two people sixty miles, which equals 120 pmpg (people miles per gallon), whereas your behemoth can seat thirteen (some comfortably—the others have seatbelts), which means on a gallon of gas you're moving thirteen people ten miles, which equals 130 pmpg. Do the math.

HANG THE EXPENSE

There is no more surprisingly difficult handyman project than to hang a door. Unless you are an absolute expert at it, the only trouble-free method for the weekend carpenter is to buy all pre-hung doors and build the house around them. But let's say we're way past that, because you've already hung a door and now you're dealing with the consequences. Here are some tips to help you solve several different problems that arise from a poorly hung door.

When you open the door, it rubs on the floor and eventually jams. If the door opens wide enough for people to go through before it jams on the floor, the most effective solution is to do nothing. You have a perfectly usable door with a clever built-in doorstop to hold it open while you're bringing in lumber for your next project— or while the paramedics are taking you out on a stretcher. However, if the door only opens a few inches before jamming (as in Diag. 1), you have to deal with it.

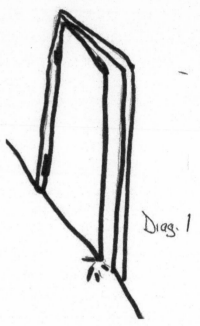

Diag. 1

This is because you hung the door with complete disregard for your two most important helpers: plumb and level. Start by measuring the angles between the floor and the door. You'll need something large and square, other than your uncle.

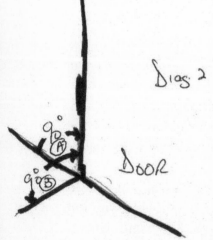

Diag. 2

Door

As shown in Diag. 2, both angles need to be exactly 90 degrees. The further you're out, the less the door will open. If you're around 65 degrees, the door may not open at all. If you're lucky and Angle A is 90 degrees but Angle B is only 85 degrees, you can correct it easily by moving either of the hinges in the door jamb until it's at a right angle. The door will then open freely. If Angle B is okay but Angle A is off, you need to add shims behind one of the hinges until it brings that angle to 90 degrees. The door will now swing freely, but there will be other adjustments required. See below.

The door now swings freely but it won't close. The shims under one of the hinges have had the effect of changing the shape of the door so that it is now slightly larger than the frame. To correct this, open the door and step through to the other side. Now pull the door towards you until it bangs up against the frame. Remove the pencil from your ear—or, if you're a true handyman, remove the pencil from *above* your ear—and draw a line where the frame touches the door. Remove the door by undoing the hinges on the door edge. Leave the frame edge alone, as removing the hinges from that side will alter the shimming effect and you'll be spending the rest of your life hanging this door. Use a saw—or, if you're lumberjack, a very sharp hatchet—to trim the door to fit the frame. Reinstall the door and it will swing freely and close without hitting the frame. However, there will be other adjustments required. See below.

The door swings freely and closes, but does not latch. The shimming and trimming have also changed the angle of the door so that the latching mechanism on the door no longer lines up with the receptacle in the frame. You may be getting a little frustrated at this point, so I suggest you take a five-pound sledgehammer and drive the latch mechanism deep into the bowels of the door. This will mean your door won't latch, but so what? If you need to keep it closed, pound a nail into the frame and bend it over so it catches the door. If you're a purist, you can move the receptacle up or down on the frame so that it lines up with the latch mechanism.

Unless the door is latched, it will not stay in place. It either swings wide open or slams shut. Here again, this is because the door is not mounted plumb and, as Dolly Parton knows, gravity isn't always your friend. The simplest solution is to put a door-stop on the low side, but then you have to move it every time you want to change the angle of the door. The second-simplest solution is to let the door swing until it comes to rest. Then look to see which corner of the house the open door is pointing to. Go outside and jack up that corner of the house until the door closes. You need to be aware that this solution may affect the performance of all of the other doors in your home.

The most complex solution is to remove the door and frame, reinstall the door inside the free-standing frame, and slide the frame into the door opening. Through trial and error, try every angle available on each of the four corners of the frame until you find the combination that allows the door to swing freely, close properly and stay in place when partially open. Bear in mind that this test will take each corner of the frame through at least a ten-degree range. Plus, there are two planes to deal with for each corner, so you have ten degrees times two for each corner—and, each of the other corners has the same number of variables for each position of the first corner. The mathematical equation for the number of combinations is 2×10^4, which means you may have to try twenty thousand different configurations before you find the one that works. Unless you're doing this job in prison as part of your community service, I suggest you see below.

Diag. 3

The best way to hang a door.
Put up a beaded curtain.

HOW TO MAKE DINNER MORE ROMANTIC

Your wife enjoys going out for dinner, of course, but the cost may negatively impact your hopes of buying a new snowmobile. Don't panic. What your wife really wants is a break from the drudgery of preparing meals, in an environment that is solicitously romantic. If you can find a way to do that without leaving your own home, you both win. Here's how.

- Start by giving her a bouquet of flowers. Then put the flowers in a vase and position them on the table so that your neighbour can't see them through the window—just in case they came from his garden.
- Make sure you both sit at the table for dinner. Very hard to have meaningful conversation while you're eating over the sink.
- Get dressed. You may think a T-shirt and sweat pants are your way of saying you're comfortable with her, but she doesn't see it that way. Put on a pair of dress pants and a shirt that doesn't have any words on it. There's no harm in being a little overdressed, even if your WIFE is wearing a T-shirt and sweat pants.
- Get the kids to go outside and play. Especially if they're not your kids.
- Light candles. (If you do your own home renovating, shut off the gas first).
- Put on some music. Instrumental. No bluegrass. No marching bands. Lots of strings and saxophones. Tempo should be between the "Death March" and "Flight of the Bumble Bee."
- Make dinner. If you don't have a microwave, you can order something in. If you order in, be sure to take the food out of the cardboard containers before serving. Especially if your candles are short.

- Serve martinis and high-end appetizers. Note: Crayfish are not a substitute for shrimp.
- Use silverware, especially if you're having soup or mashed potatoes.
- Find a clock with a second hand and mount it on the wall behind your wife's chair. When she starts talking, glance at the second hand and make sure you let her go at least two minutes without interrupting while you stare into her eyes. Keep your responses to a maximum of thirty seconds and make sure you're talking about her.
- Let her decide on the topics of conversation. Don't mention any body parts in your comments. Don't even point at them.
- Serve the salad and make sure you get the larger portion.
- Take the dirty dishes away between courses, rather than pushing them to the side or tossing them under the table. Note: Even when there are no bones, it is never okay to just lick the plates off and reuse them.
- The best choice for dessert is always chocolate. Every woman loves chocolate. Just be sure to remove the bars from their wrappers.
- Insist on doing all the cleanup while she relaxes in the living room. Your wife will appreciate that you're going to do the dishes and put the leftovers away, but the main advantage for you is that it prevents her from seeing what you've done to her kitchen.
- Once the kitchen is cleaned up, take your wife out for a walk. It's healthy, it's romantic and it's cheap. And if there are any digestive issues arising from your meal, it's probably better for everyone if you're outdoors.
- My guess is that if you do this properly, your wife will appreciate the gesture and give you full points for

effort while quietly doing everything in her power to make sure it doesn't happen again for a long, long time.

SEVEN LEGAL THINGS YOU CAN DO WITH A DAMP BASEMENT

Many of us who live in older homes have the recurring problem of a damp basement. Maybe there's something wrong with the drainage of the yard, or maybe the home was built accidentally below sea level—or maybe, when the foundation was waterproofed, they used an inferior brand of duct tape. In any case, trying to fix a damp basement can be frustrating and expensive. Instead, here are a few cheap creative suggestions.

1) Several cash crops flourish in a damp environment. If your basement is only somewhat damp, I would recommend shiitake mushrooms. If it's really wet down there, go with wild rice.

2) Why spend hundreds of dollars going to a fancy spa when you can just open the furnace door, crank up the heat and turn your damp basement into a sauna?

3) Many craftsmen who build canoes or stair banisters need a damp environment to allow the wood to bend easily. Rent them your basement during their busy season, and then when they move out, use the money to buy a dehumidifier.

4) Airflow is a great cure for excessive dampness—as anybody knows who's ever wet their pants on a windy day. Open your basement windows. If they're swollen shut from the dampness, you may have to jack the house up just a little. Open them up wide and then buy a used jet engine on eBay. Disconnect your furnace and connect all the fuel lines and the chimney flue directly to the jet engine.

You may not get full speed using heating oil, but the jet will still run fast enough to pull a lot of dry air through your basement. The damp air will be expelled at high speed through your chimney and will form a small rain cloud, which will then head for Vancouver. Make sure you take all the furniture out of the basement before trying this. Nothing good happens when a leatherette recliner is sucked through a jet turbine.

5) Dampness creates mould, and mould creates penicillin. Don't think of it as a wet basement; think of it as a generic pharmacy.

6) Anyone who makes their own bread knows that once the yeast is added to the dough, it needs to rest in a warm, damp environment to rise properly. Remove all the side panels from your furnace, exposing the high-volume burner, and voila, you can make the dough and bake the bread right there. Try to imagine the size of the loaves you could make when you have your whole basement as the oven. But you have to eventually bring the super-loaves up to the dining room, so don't make them too big, especially if your basement stairs have a turn in them.

7) I don't know about you, but I've always wanted to be able to have a late-night campfire in the comfort of my own home. It not only brings the family together, it's a great way to meet your local firemen. That's due to the ever-present danger of setting your house on fire. You've seen it on TV, where one house is on fire and the firemen are hosing down the house next door. Well, why not take a page out of their book? Your leaky basement is getting hosed down on a daily basis. It's not gonna catch fire. So gather up some firewood, bring your guitar, your sleeping bag and the smores and head down to the basement campfire. Heck, if you build it over the sewer drain, you can use the methane as fire-starter.

QUICK TIP #3: CAR PULLS TO THE LEFT

If you let go of the steering wheel and your car pulls one way or the other, that's a sign that you need a front-end alignment. And, as in every situation that leads to words you're not familiar with, like "camber" and "caster," you just know it's going to be expensive. A cheaper solution if, say, your car pulls to the left, is to let 25 per cent of the air out of the right front tire. Problem solved.

MULTIPLE-CHOICE SENSITIVE-MAN QUIZ

There was a time when a man was the centre of his universe and everyone else in the family was expected to alter their behaviour and attitudes so that they would fall in line with his wishes. Sadly, those days are gone and are not coming back. So the best way for us to now move forward is to make sure we have evolved into the kind of sensitive, caring individuals that make this a more pleasant and more just world for everyone else who is in it with us. Here's a short sensitivity quiz so you can measure your progress.

1) What do you answer when your wife asks, "Does this dress make me look fat?"
   a) "No, but it's a bit out of style. Why don't you go out and get yourself something new?"—25 points

b) "Compared to which other dress?"—15 points

c) "Don't worry, nobody will be looking."—10 points

d) "I don't think it's fair to blame the dress."—0 points

2) What is the best way to rebuild your truck's engine?

   a) Taking the truck to a licensed mechanic at a service centre.—25 points

   b) Having a friend do it in his garage.—15 points

   c) Doing it *with* a friend in *your* garage.—10 points

   d) Doing it by yourself on the dining room table.—0 points

3) Something's come up and you know you're going to be coming home from work late. What do you do?

   a) Phone home and tell your wife that you're going to be late and ask her if she'd like to go out to a nice restaurant for a late dinner.—25 points

   b) Phone home and tell her not to wait up.—15 points

   c) Don't phone home, on the basis that it saves you a double dose of complaints—one when you call and the other when you finally arrive.—10 points

   d) Don't phone, and after the extra work is done, go for a drink with your co-workers in an attempt to arrive home so late that your wife is too tired to be angry.—0 points.

4) Your neighbour borrowed your lawn mower and returned it broken. What do you do?

   a) Suck it up and say nothing.—25 points

   b) Take it back and ask him to fix it.—15 points

   c) Borrow his weed whacker and return it in pieces. —10 points

   d) Kill his lawn.—0 points

5) Your son comes home with a large metal stud in his nose. What do you do?

a) Compliment him on his individuality and ask if it was painful.—25 points
b) Ask him if this means he's ruled out the priesthood. —15 points
c) While he's asleep, attach a tissue to his nose with a fridge magnet.—10 points
d) Sprinkle his dinner with pepper.—0 points

6) When do you think it's okay for you to have your shirt off?
a) While showering, swimming underwater or during a lunar eclipse.—25 points
b) While working in the yard.—15 points
c) During a meal.—10 points
d) At your arraignment.—0 points

7) What does the date February 14 mean to you?
a) St. Valentine's Day.—25 points
b) Start of the NCAA playoffs.—15 points
c) Opening of the seal hunt.—10 points
d) Anniversary of your incarceration.—0 points

8) You've just been pulled over by a cop for speeding. What do you do?
a) Admit that you weren't paying enough attention to your speed and apologize to the police officer.—25 points
b) Suggest that, in the interest of safety, you were going the same speed as the rest of the traffic.—15 points
c) Deny any wrongdoing and insist that he's had an equipment malfunction.—10 points
d) Make fun of his hat.—0 points

9) Today is your wedding anniversary. What do you do?
a) Arrive home with a romantic card, chocolates, flowers and an expensive gift.—25 points

b) Arrive home with tickets to the monster truck rally. —15 points

c) Arrive home with nothing.—10 points

d) Don't arrive home.—0 points

HOW TO DRESS

The first challenge in getting most men to dress properly is getting them to care. The best way to do this is with negative feedback, which can be a powerful motivating factor in persuading a man to improve the way he presents himself to the world. This negativity can come from a variety of sources. Perhaps his boss points out that the way the man dresses is one of the reasons—along with his lack of personality, ambition and high school diploma—he is not being promoted. Maybe his local bar introduces a dress code. Maybe his wife stops feeding him until he puts his pants on.

I've noticed that old guys tend, on average, to dress better than young guys. That means that being better dressed is inevitable, so why not start now? With a small amount of time and money and a few simple rules, you too can start looking better and achieve that rich, rewarding personal and professional success that has been eluding you these past forty-seven years.

The most important step is to accept that each human being is unique, each with our strengths and weaknesses, which means clothes that look good on one man may not look on another. For example, a Speedo may look okay if your stomach is a six-pack, but not if it's a case of twenty-four with a side order of curly fries. So start by evaluating which parts of your appearance are assets and which are liabilities. You wife can be very helpful in this area, but have her inform you just a bit at a time. Hearing it all at once can result in an emotional tailspin that drops you back into your sweatpants and keeps you there. For the purposes of our discussion, let's say you're an average-looking middle-aged guy: somewhat overweight, balding, you don't shave every day and you're bitter after seeing the results of basing your life on pure luck. Here are a few things you can do to make yourself more attractive to the ladies, and some of the men.

Nudist camps have proven that the human eye is drawn to the biggest thing on a person. This is not always good. On most middle-aged guys, despite what they say, the biggest thing they're carrying around is their gut. Now, you could go on a diet and exercise regimen to trim that area down, but who are we kidding here? Instead, you have to balance your look by adding something just as large. Let's say, for example, that your waist measurement is fifty-two inches. Dividing that number by 3.14, or pi (probably one of many pies associated with the problem), gives you a core diameter of sixteen inches. That means you need to have a shoulder width of at least twenty-four inches to get a pleasing, V-shaped body. You can do this with expensive cosmetic surgery, or maybe just pick up a pair of shoulder pads at the Joan Crawford garage sale. (If shoulder enhancement is too expensive because it involves buying all new T-shirts, you could opt for a cowboy hat with a brim thirty-six inches in diameter. But that comes with a whole other set of problems, starting with the standard door width of thirty-two inches.) The main point is, you have to diminish the dominance of your largest feature by balancing it with something equally big. If you'd rather balance your stomach with something *below* the waistline, maybe clown shoes would be appropriate.

Symmetry is also important. You want each side of your body to look the same. If your right knee is large and knobby from all those years of kicking the screen door open when you enter with a case of beer in each hand, balance them up by duct-taping a tennis ball to your left knee. Just remember not to wear shorts. Speaking of shorts, they only look good when their length is greater than their width. Once you've broken that barrier, shorts are no longer an option. If your waist measurement ever becomes larger than your inseam, you may have to wear pants that are much too long for you and cover it by standing on stilts.

The main objective in trying to make yourself look thinner is to find ways to take away your roundness. Round things look fat. You need long, narrow things hanging vertically to offset the roundness. Slimming accessories include a long beard, a pony-tail, a scarf, a stovepipe hat, a noose or a knee-length tie.

If you're at a party or a social gathering, you can use the furniture and the floor plan to help you look slimmer. A tall wing-back chair is a great thing to stand behind. As long as your head is visible, you can participate in conversation and meaningful eye contact. Similarly, if you can hang back at the entrance and stand so that your body is never completely inside the room, the other guests will, in time, assume that they're seeing all of you.

Long, flowing clothes are a time-honoured disguise for obesity. Orson Welles, Barry White and Mama Cass were all proponents of the "waterfall look." It would be more helpful to think of people who are still alive, but there aren't very many.

Probably the most effective tool in looking fit is talking fit. Talk about how you spent the day surfing—don't mention you were using the TV remote. Tell about how you can bench press 275 pounds—don't say you do it by standing up when the bus comes. These tricks are much easier to pull off with acquaintances, so avoid making friends.

Maintain a positive attitude. A happy, confident personality will override any fashion deficiencies; embrace rather than deny your bigness, your magnificence, your enormous-iosity. Think of all the positive things that come out of being huge—nobody expects you to do anything quickly, you are safe in high wind conditions, people are drawn to you through gravitational pull, everyone else is afraid to take the last cookie, and your friends want you to outlive them just so they can avoid being pallbearers.

HOW TO SURVIVE AN OFFICE JOB

The key to having a successful career in an office environment is to have a realistic expectation of what goals are achievable or even desirable. At the top end, you have the CEO, who is obsessive and drinking heavily as he tries to figure out how to cope with the stress of being able to afford his lifestyle. At the bottom end, you'll find a guy who got fired for incompetence and is now destitute and drinking heavily as he tries to figure out how to cope with the stress of being able to afford his lifestyle. Where you want to be is somewhere between those two extremes. But it's not easy. You want to be doing just enough work not to get fired, but not enough that you're given any responsibility. Along with this approach, you must accept that you are never going to ask for a salary increase. Instead, you're going to focus your efforts on getting what I call a Canadian raise—the same pay for less work. Here are a few tips to take you to the middle and keep you there.

Take a close look at the position before you accept it. If it comes with a detailed job description and regular employee reviews, this is clearly not the place for you. You're looking for a disorganized management regime where nobody really knows who does what or how anything gets done.

Learn how to look busy. Have a messy desk, but a neat and full filing cabinet. Take papers from one to the other and back again at regular intervals. Make sure you get a lot of phone calls. Give your number to telemarketers, and when they call, be gruff and authoritative with them so that fellow workers will think you're the man. Never saunter anywhere. Walk with a purpose, particularly when you don't have one. Use the restroom that's the farthest from your desk. It'll give you a place to go.

Create the perception of competence while avoiding commitment. Avoid speaking at office meetings. Look like you're completely focused on what everyone is saying. Make your head movements almost imperceptible and therefore ambiguous. When cornered for your opinion, say, "No matter what we decide to do, it won't work without a consensus, so the feelings of the majority are more important than mine." But don't say that every time, especially not word for word. Then, just as they ask for a show of hands, drop something on the floor so you can do a quick count while you're picking it up, ensuring you're always able to vote with the majority. This will make you appear to be a team player. If the idea works, you'll be one of the guys who supported it. If the idea fails, it wasn't yours.

Be a company guy. Go to all the company parties and always propose a toast to management. If the company has any promotional clothing, buy it and wear it to work. Paint the company logo on your car. Post all positive company memos, like announcements of new contracts or quarterly reports, on the cafeteria bulletin board under a WAY TO GO banner. Strongly disagree with any employee who criticizes the company, unless said employee is your superior.

Be emotional. When complimented, almost hug the person. Cry when criticized. Bring flowers into the office.

Survive through surveillance. You need to keep a close eye on the number of employees. If you're surviving using the steps described above, it means your company is the ideal size for this specific approach to office work. If they take on more employees, you will become expendable. If they shrink the roster, there will be fewer people covering for you and you'll be gone.

HOW TO WORK TIRELESSLY

One of the most onerous expenses facing today's hobbyist auto mechanic is the high price of tire disposal. There is no greater insult than the wrecker telling you that not only will he not give you any cash for your car, but he also needs ten bucks to dispose of the tires. Doesn't it make more sense to find useful, creative applications that help the environment and add property value? This is an opportunity just waiting to be exploited. How? Here are some possibilities.

A TRIBUTE TO THE OLYMPICS

What better way to salute the great Olympic tradition than by recreating the five Olympic rings on your shed wall? Even better if you have white-walls, because that will allow you to paint the appropriate colour on each tire. And you can get all five tires from one car as long as you have a spare.

THE TREE HUGGER

Here's a nifty way to help Mother Nature defend herself against the garbage trucks and school buses that are forever bouncing off that tree you planted maybe a little too close to the road. You're saving the tree *and* greatly reducing the damage to the vehicles—unless they bounce off the tree and hit the cement culvert that you built maybe a little too high.

GIMME SHELTER

You're not going to find a cheaper, more resilient bus shelter than a stack of steel-belted radials. Cut small square holes out of the tread of each tire so that the kids can climb up the outside; then, after they drop down inside, they can use the footholds as little windows to watch out for the school bus. And, surrounding them with the pungent aroma of used tires will stop them from eating their lunch while they're waiting.

A DECORATIVE WREATH

If you have a well-built solid front door, you can hang a beautiful tire on it. You can even change it to match the weather, using a rain tire or snow tire or, if you prefer low mainte-nance, an all-season truck tire. A tire on your front door is not only a friendly tribute to travelling salesmen, it's also a subtle way of wishing your neighbours a Goodyear.

WHEN YOUR NUMBER'S UP

If you want a unique and distinctive look for your home, use as many tires as necessary to recreate your street number on the front wall of your house. It will be large and easy to read—except at night, but you don't want people coming over after dark anyway. The only possible limitation is that your address can only have eights and zeros in it. Or you can just make up an address and use that. As long as your friends think they're looking for house number 8088, they'll find you, no problem. Who cares if it throws off the mailman? He won't be able to deliver the bills.

IMPORTANT RESEARCH FOR THE DO-IT-YOURSELFER

If you're the kind of person who is independently minded and fearless and is always looking for the best value to the point of being almost cheap, I'm about to give you some very good advice. It doesn't really matter what the specific project is, the advice stays the same, as does the procedure. But for the purposes of this example, let's say your roof needs to be reshingled and you've had three quotes, none of which you find particularly exciting, so now you've decided to do the job yourself. You'll just go at your own pace and save a lot of money.

Okay, before you whip your shirt off and strap on your tool belt, there are a few steps you need to take. First of all, determine what tools are necessary to reshingle a roof. You'll need a crowbar to pry off the old shingles. A crowbar is a simple tool, so there shouldn't be any problems there. However, you'll need a hammer to nail the new shingles down. This is a little more complicated because, over time, the head on a hammer can get quite loose. So when the head flies off your hammer, you'll have to come all the way down to retrieve it from where it's lying on the ground beside your unconscious neighbour. And, any savings on the roofing job will be more than absorbed by the legal costs once he comes to. So you need a good hammer. Similarly, you won't want to compromise as far as your ladder's concerned.

If you've had that same wooden ladder for over twenty years, chances are it's lost even more integrity than you have. You need a good ladder.

Now let's get a little more personal. Think of the vertigo you get when you climb up on a chair to take your underwear off the ceiling fan. Well, it's a pretty good bet that the roof of your house is significantly higher than any of your ceiling fans. So maybe you should just try climbing the ladder empty-handed and see how far you get before you freeze up and your wife has to call the fire department to bring you back down. Now let's add the fitness component. Put a bundle of shingles on your shoulder and see if you can even stand up, much less climb a ladder. Oh sure, you could take one shingle at a time, but that's a lot of trips. And judging from your profile, you'd still be doing a lot of heavy lifting.

Now we get to the core of the issue. You think you're just as good, if not better, at reshingling your roof as anybody who does it for a living? Let's find out. Go down to your local roofing company and ask the guy if there's anybody in there doing roof work who looks like you. He'll say no. Now drop into the emergency room of your local hospital and ask the receptionist the same question, and you'll get an entirely different response.

TWELVE WAYS TO LIVEN UP A PARTY

No matter how interesting your friends may be, parties are a lot more fun when you break the ice and get everybody to loosen up a little. Here are twelve ways to do just that.

1) Serve cocktails in glasses made of ice. It forces your guests to drink faster.
2) Set up a large terrarium and leave the lid wide open. Put a sign on it saying SNAKES: KEEP LID CLOSED.

3) Hire an unemployed CIA agent to secretly record all kitchen conversations from the first two hours of the party, edit them down to the good stuff and then play back the edited version for a fun-filled exposé of how your guests really feel about each other.

4) Make a large wet spot in the carpet just outside the powder room door.

5) For background music, play a CD of dishes breaking, fistfights, drive-by shootings, fire trucks and women screaming.

6) Hide bacon in all the chairs and bring in a stray dog.

7) Have a couple of cops arrive, put you in cuffs and escort you out. (Only do this if you think it will surprise your guests.)

8) Insert small firecrackers into the candles.

9) Hire a clown and give everyone a full seltzer bottle.

10) Bury a rubber mouse in the bottom of the cheese dip.

11) Play a game where everybody tries to line the guests up in descending order of net worth.

12) Rig the toilet handle so that when it's flushed, a flashbulb goes off.

WHY WE HAVE RULES

The vast majority of rules you see everywhere in life are based on experience—something bad happened, so a rule was created to prevent that bad thing from ever happening again.

So the next time you're at a public place or in a factory, take a look at the rules posted on the walls and signposts and try to pick out the ones that were created after the accident. Here are a few to practise on.

- GIRLS WITH PIGTAILS SHOULD STAND WELL BACK FROM THE LATHE
- ATTENTION PIZZA TOSSERS: DO NOT STAND UNDER THE CEILING FAN
- DOGS ON LEASHES ARE NOT ALLOWED TO RIDE TILT-A-WHIRL
- ZEBRA MUSSEL WARNING: NO NUDE SWIMMING
- UNICYCLE WEIGHT RESTRICTION—200 LBS. OPERATOR NOT RESPONSIBLE FOR REMOVING UNICYCLE FROM BODY ORIFICE
- ENDANGERED BIRD SANCTUARY: NO CATS ALLOWED
- METHANE COLLECTION AREA—NO LOITERING, NO PICNICS, NO CANDLES
- LIVE PEREGRINE FALCON: DO NOT STICK YOUR TONGUE THROUGH PROTECTIVE FENCE
- BURIED NATURAL GAS PIPELINE—POGO STICKS PROHIBITED
- THIN ICE: CALL 911 AT LEAST FIFTEEN MINUTES BEFORE DRIVING YOUR VEHICLE ON THE LAKE
- HIGH WIND ON MOUNTAIN: WATCH FOR FALLING SMART CARS
- WATCH FOR SQUIRRELS: DO NOT CARRY FOOD IN PANTS POCKETS
- HIGH-VOLTAGE POWER TRANSFORMER IN PICNIC AREA: FOIL-WRAPPED POTATOES MAY EXPLODE
- STEEP GRADE: IF YOUR TRAILER WEIGHS MORE THAN YOUR VEHICLE, GO UP THE HILL BACKWARDS
- ARCHERY RANGE: DO NOT WEAR CLOTHING THAT FEATURES CIRCLES
- SPIDER MIGRATION AREA: TUCK PANTLEGS INTO SOCKS
- IDIOT ZONE: IF YOU'RE SMART, YOU'LL LEAVE

MAKING ALTERNATIVE FUEL

If you own an air compressor, you can make your own alternative fuel. An air compressor works by taking in air through the filtered inlet pipe (see diagram) and pumping it into a collection tank.

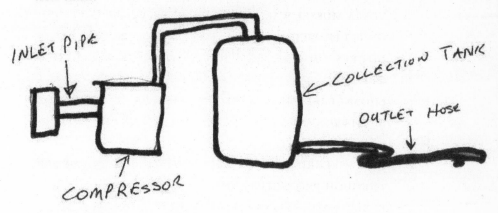

As the pump runs, pressure builds up in the tank and eventually reaches the point where the air can be discharged forcefully through the nozzle on the outlet hose. All you need is a source of combustible gas that you can channel into the compressor and use as a delivery mechanism for your car's modified fuel tank (also known as an empty propane tank).

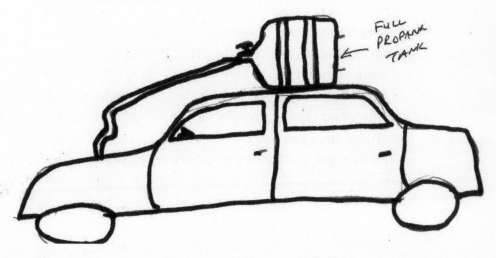

So when you're looking for a readily available, environmentally friendly combustible gas, what's the first thing that comes to mind? That's right, methane. For those of you who are lucky enough to have a septic system, you have a virtually limitless supply of methane, especially if you also have a large family. In fact, every time you use the facility, you are sitting on a gold mine. And it's so easy to do. Take a length of vacuum cleaner hose and duct tape one end, so that it's airtight, around the filter on the compressor intake. Dangle the other end into the upper chamber of your septic tank. Be careful not to go too deep into the tank—I'd rather not say why. Now start up the compressor and the methane will be pumped and compressed into the pressure tank.

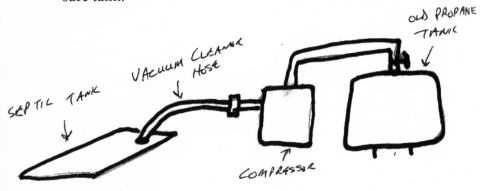

You can test whether or not you have enough methane concentration by spraying the nozzle over an open flame. You should get a large blue flame, and ideally one that smells like an outhouse on fire. Use the compressed methane to fill up the empty propane tank, which now becomes the gas tank for your car. Hook it up to the engine's intake manifold and you're on your way to free, eco-friendly driving. As a bonus, the smell of the exhaust will put an end to tailgating.

ITEMS THAT DON'T MIX

In nature, as in life, there are certain things that just don't go well together. This is less of a problem in nature because natural enemies don't stay together for long. In life, incompatibility isn't always so obvious. So to help in that regard, here's a list of things that should never be together:

- bright lights and toupees
- laxatives and tuba solos
- alcohol and nuclear devices
- nude beaches and binoculars
- weddings and former fiancées
- riding mowers and gravel driveways
- topless dancers and pogo sticks
- Christmas dinners and belt buckles
- the stock market and your money
- firecrackers and nearsighted cigar smokers
- a suit of armour and lightning
- dog biscuits in your pants pocket and a dachshund
- wedding nights and video cameras
- greenhouses and golf balls
- Viagra and solitary confinement

QUICK TIP #4: OPENING A STICKY DOOR

On the outside, leave a pitchfork resting up against a nearby wall. You'll find that the tines of the pitchfork will slide easily under the doorknob, and then you can just lean against the pitchfork handle to pry the door open. If the doorknob is not attached securely, you'll find out right away. On the inside, mount the flat side of a hockey puck on the door about eighteen inches below the doorknob. Put on your line-dancing cowboy boots and boot-scoot your heel up to the puck with extreme prejudice. You can practise the motion by kick-starting a motorcycle on a steep hill.

HOW TO TELL IF YOU'RE TOO FOCUSED ON YOUR JOB

In the old days, putting your nose to the grindstone and burning the midnight oil would lead to success in business, which was ultimately the best thing you could do for yourself and your loved ones. But now that having any kind of success is virtually impossible, the goal is to lead a more balanced life that allows you time to appreciate your friends and family. To make that happen, you must be prepared to ease off a bit on the career front. You have a finite amount of time and energy, and if you're going to spend more of each with family and friends, it has to come from somewhere, and your job is the obvious choice. Unfortunately for the small minority of people who don't work for the government or don't belong to a labour union, slacking off may not be easy. Nonetheless, the first step in addressing any problem is to acknowledge it. Here are the danger signs that indicate you are too focused on your job.

- You are making significantly more money than you did when you started working for the company.
- You carry a BlackBerry and always have it turned on.
- The boss knows you by your first name.
- You handle the company's major accounts.
- You have a company car and the keys to the company ski chalet, even though you never get enough time off to go there.
- Your boss told you an extremely personal secret, and now you can't help but notice how much the receptionist's baby looks like him.
- When you're handed your paycheque, you say thank you.
- You have never pretended to be sick and have often pretended to be well.
- You wear a company windbreaker a lot, even though the dancing-panda logo is a little effeminate.
- You have a drink with the boss whenever he asks you, and he's a drunk.
- You dream about how the company could be run better.
- When friends are looking for you, they call your work number first.
- Your wife no longer sets a place for you at the table.
- Your kids look like your boss.

HOW YOUR POOL CAN SHOVEL SNOW

If you live in a colder climate and you have a backyard swimming pool, here's an idea that's going to make you look brilliant (and believe me, they're few and far between).

Every year when winter comes, you drain the pool down a few feet and throw logs in to absorb the expansion when the surface freezes. You also contract with somebody to plow the snow out of your driveway. Well, here's a way to use one thing to replace the other. In a colder climate, a swimming pool isn't the best investment in the first place, so anything you can do to increase efficiency may reduce the pain of having one. Often in life we find that a ridiculous decision can make a silly one look smart.

So in the summer when the ground is soft, bury a couple of hundred feet of garden hose about six inches deep in your driveway. Hook the garden hose up to your pool pump. Put a valve on there so you can keep it shut off during the warm months (or weeks, or days, depending on how far north you are). When winter comes, drain the pool as usual and throw in the logs, because I know you really enjoy that part, but set up the pump so that it circulates water from the bottom of the pool through the buried garden hose. In a swimming pool, only the surface freezes, so the water will be able to run all winter, keeping your driveway a few degrees above the freezing point and melting the snow as it lands.

Think of all the money you'll save by not needing anyone to plow your driveway. And if you're concerned about the cost of running the pump all winter, run an extension cord from your neighbour's house. It's a win-win.

IMPORTANT LIFE LESSONS

One of the things I can do to help my fellow man (and I'm hoping this will be counted towards my assigned hours of community service) is to pass on any valuable life lessons that I've had so that you don't have to go through the pain and embarrassment of learning them first-hand. So here's a list of proven facts from my own experience, just in case you were considering trying any of this stuff.

- Do not sneeze into a bowl of coffee creamer near an open flame.
- If weed killer is not diluted with water as described on the box, your lawn will die.
- An automatic garage door does not have enough power to lift even a small-block V8.
- Driving really, really fast on a flat tire will not generate enough centrifugal force to make it round again.
- Never drink hot coffee without your pants on.
- Deodorant does not work after the fact.
- Never confuse facts with opinions. When a person says, "He's my dog," that's a fact. When a person says, "He won't bite," that's an opinion.
- There are many problems you can put off till another day, but a sewage leak isn't one of them.
- Married men never get away with anything.
- The oil dipstick is there for a reason.
- If you've been smelling propane for more than five minutes, don't keep pressing the sparker.
- They call it softwood, but it's still harder than a human head.
- Nose hair is flammable.
- If you've had a beard for more than five years, you should never, ever shave it off.

- Don't use any recreational or fitness device if the picture on the box shows a guy your son's age.
- Always live within walking distance of the hospital . . . and the fire station.
- Never take advice from anybody who's never done anything—present company excluded.

LESS IS MOWER

There are many things that can ruin a Saturday. The main one, of course, is realizing that it's actually Wednesday. But aside from that, the biggest disappointment is knowing you have to cut the lawn. This is something that may be pointed out to you by your significant other, or that becomes clear to you when you can no longer see out any of the windows. Oh sure, I know you have a gas mower that's pretty easy to use once you get it started and the pain in your shoulder subsides to the point that you can move your arm again, and you've accepted the practice of tilting it up every few feet to let the clogged grass spew out into your above-ground pool, and you're even okay with the odd rock the mower picks up and fires into your neighbour's trampoline and then who knows where. But I'm thinking there must be a better way. And there is.

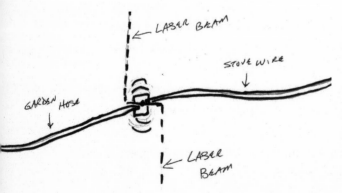

Step One: Pick up a couple of laser-beam generators. You can get them cheap from any of those do-it-yourself eye-surgery websites. Laser generators generally run on 110-volt current, but for our application you'll need more power, so you should hook them up to your stove outlet.

Step Two: Once you've got those wired up, attach the lasers to the bottom edges of an old-fashioned rotary lawn sprinkler. You'll need enough electrical cable and hose to be able to put the sprinkler dead centre in your lawn. Even if it's not exactly dead centre, it soon will be.

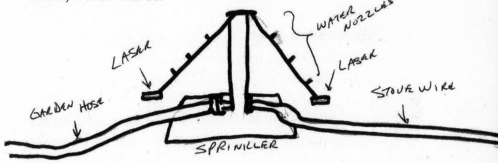

Step Three: Turn on the water, which will get the sprinkler rotating.

Step Four: Put on a full-body rubber wet suit and rubber gloves and stand on a thick rubber mat while you turn on the power switch.

And it's just that simple. In less than ten rotations, your lawn will be cut perfectly flat and the clippings will be incinerated.

Finally, turn off the power, then the water, and stay off the lawn until it's completely dry to avoid any residual electrical energy that could impede your ability to grow hair.

CAUTION: Do not use near flower gardens or house pets.

Grain farmers should ask about the military-grade laser beam, capable of harvesting a hundred acres per hour.

PEOPLE WHO SHOULDN'T DRINK COFFEE

- Eye Surgeons
- Anger-Management Counsellors
- Bomb Defusers
- Funeral Directors
- Flagpole Sitters
- Proctologists
- Complaint-Desk Clerks
- Executioners
- Tightrope Walkers
- Nitroglycerine Deliverymen
- Hernia Testers

TEN REASONS TO HAVE A GRAVEL DRIVEWAY

1) **Drainage.** Gravel allows any spilled liquid to drain through and sink into the ground rather than forming a small toxic river that heads straight for your basement windows. It even filters the stuff as it passes through. It's an ideal component for anyone who operates a still or has a leaky gas tank or pet.

2) **Lack of bounceability.** It is virtually impossible to play basketball on a gravel driveway. This will save you from having to buy a backboard and hoop and then spend your days yelling at teenagers. The only dunking done at your house will be in the kitchen, with a dozen honey crullers.

3) **Ammunition.** How many times have you seen an animal digging up your vegetables, or a bird sitting on your car, and wished you could pick up a stone and wing it? With a gravel driveway, you can make that dream a reality. And

you can even call the resultant crack in your windshield a stone chip and get it covered by your car insurance.

4) **Security.** One of the great properties of gravel is its ability to be mounded—something you don't see in an asphalt driveway unless you went with the lowest tender. This "moundability," as it's called in the industry, allows you to build a gravel berm around your vehicle, your compost heap, your inverted motor home or any valuables that are dangerously vulnerable sitting out in your front yard. The gravel barrier will make your stuff virtually impossible to steal. Any thief is much more likely to swipe your neighbour's inverted motor home.

5) **Sustainability.** As long as you carry a bucket in your trunk, you will have an endless supply of gravel to replace any that's lost over the years. Pavement is an all-or-nothing situation; gravel is modular by nature, and as long as you stay away from the coloured varieties, you can use virtually any size or shape to go along with what's already there. You will find that every kind of gravel you bring home will match—particularly if that's how you made the driveway in the first place.

6) **Privacy.** If you have lots of gravel and a backhoe, you can make huge mounds that prevent passersby from seeing your home, your garage, your vehicle or your stolen backhoe.

7) **Guest-arrival alert.** There is absolutely no way for a vehicle to come into a gravel driveway quietly. And that extra ten or fifteen seconds' warning you get when unexpected visitors arrive is often just long enough to comb your hair and put your pants on.

8) **Inertness.** Gravel is rock in a manageable size, so it tends to be virtually impervious to chemicals, heat or impact. So don't worry about any gasoline spills or the resultant fireball—the driveway will be fine. Same thing when you

fall off your roof; even if you land on something hard, like your head, the gravel will remain unscathed.

9) **Low maintenance.** The first clue as to how easy it is to maintain a gravel driveway is the manual—there isn't one. Sometimes there's a very small piece of paper that says, "Do nothing. Ever." It's a little larger in Canada, because it also has to say, "*Ne fais rien. Jamais.*"

10) **Flexibility.** This is the ultimate perk: the ability to move your driveway anywhere you want. All it takes is a shovel and a weekend. You can even make a circular driveway that forces visitors to go right back out without ever coming anywhere near your house. And if you make a mistake with gravel, you can always correct it. With pavement mistakes, there's always blame. That's why they call it "asphalt."

REDUCING YOUR CARBON FOOTPRINT

There has been a lot of talk lately about how we humans are destroying our planet with global warming. Al Gore has done a lot to try to reduce our carbon footprints and enlarge his own shadow.

A carbon footprint is basically the amount of carbon our lifestyle releases into the atmosphere. The main source of carbon is the gases produced when things are burned—especially fossil fuels—so before we get to the solutions, let's clearly identify the problem.

Most people think that the car is the biggest offender, and that may be true, but you have to look at all your internal combustion engines, not just the gas hog you drive to work everyday. What about your riding mower and your leaf blower and your weed whacker and your chainsaw and your log splitter and your snowmobile and your outboard motor and your ATV and your Sea-Doo and your snow blower and your Bobcat?

That two-cylinder micro-mini hybrid you drive isn't going to make up for all that other stuff, so let's have a little humility and accept that we have to make sacrifices to get this done.

As a general rule, if something is burning, we have a problem. Everything that burns produces carbon—gas, oil, propane, kerosene, your barn. And the rules change depending on where you live. For those of us who get our electricity from Niagara Falls, a candle is more harmful to the environment than turning on a light. For those who get their juice from coal-fired generators, the opposite is true. If your house is cold, don't turn on the furnace. Don't start a fire or light up a space heater. Put on a sweater. If you're still cold, revert to the laws of nature. The central source of heat in your home should be in the bedroom, not the basement. Throw a bunch of extra blankets on top, hop in and wait for your wife to run out of options.

Remember that everything in life is a trade-off. So our attempts to correct one problem will eventually create others. If we start flying by hot-air balloon rather than by airplane, we'll reduce our carbon footprint but increase our helium one. In time, we will all talk like Munchkins. There is no easy answer. Even riding a horse increases your methane footprint.

The best solution is to not need energy. If the weather's good and you don't need to go anywhere, you can reduce your carbon footprint to almost zero. So I suggest you move to Bermuda and run an Internet business from a fruit tree right next to the liquor store.

HOW TO SET UP YOUR HOME ENTERTAINMENT SYSTEM

Now that nobody over the age of forty ever goes out in the evening anymore (and who could blame them), the demand for high-quality home entertainment systems has gone through the roof. There are some good deals out there, but many people are intimidated by the challenge of hooking everything up so that it works properly. Fear no more. Here's a simple step-by-step approach to getting all of your home entertainment equipment to work together in perfect audio/visual harmony.

1) Do everything to the letter. Identify your HDTV, your PVR, your DVD player, your VHS VCR and your surround-sound RCVR.

2) Run your cable wire into a two-way splitter that will allow you to run RF lines to your PVR and your HDTV. Connect these splitter wires to the coaxial inputs of each of them (see photo #1). If you're on an antenna rather than cable, take everything back to the store and buy a Ping Pong table.

Photo #1

3) In addition to the RF line from the splitter into the HDTV, you also need to run $Y_R Y_B Y_G$ cables from the output of your PVR into the corresponding component video inputs on the HDTV (see photo #2). Run stereo audio lines from the adjacent audio jacks to connect the PVR audio output to the HDTV audio input. Make a mental note of which

component input you're using. (If a mental note is too risky, use an *actual* note.)

Photo #2

4) Similarly, run the $Y_R Y_B Y_G$ cables from the output of your DVD player to another component input on your HDTV. If you don't have a second component input, you can use an S-video cable (see photo #3). Connect the stereo audio cable as in Step 3, but do it from the DVD player to the other HDTV audio input.

Photo #3

5) Using a composite video line and stereo audio cables, connect the output of the VHS VCR to a composite input and corresponding audio inputs on the HDTV (see photo #2).

6) To get the full effect of your surround sound, you do not want the TV speakers to be on at all. In the setup menu of your HDTV, there should be a way to have the audio output unaffected by the TV volume control. (If there isn't, you're either an idiot or you went for the cheap model and now you're paying the price.) Once you set the audio output, turn the TV volume all the way down and leave it there. You want your sound to come out of the six-way surround-sound speakers, not the TV. Even if you can't understand what people are saying, it's still better quality audio than what you'd get from the TV.

7) Run audio cables from the main audio output of the HDTV into the audio input of the surround-sound RCVR (see photo #2).

8) There should also be monitor outputs on the HDTV. (If there aren't, see disciplinary note in Step 6.) Run composite video and stereo audio lines from the HDTV monitor outputs to the composite video and stereo audio inputs on the VCR (see photo #2). This will allow you to record any hi-def program or DVD signal onto a really crappy VHS tape.

9) Place your six surround-sound speakers around the room: one on each side at the front, one in the centre front, one on each side at the back, and the sub-woofer can go anywhere in the room, but they tend to overheat in bright light, so I suggest you stick it where the sun don't shine.

10) Using the speaker wire, connect each speaker to the appropriately labelled speaker output on the surround-sound RCVR. If the output says RIGHT FRONT, connecting that to the LEFT REAR speaker is just annoying (see photo #2). This completes the connection of all of your equipment.

For those of you who were paying attention, you may be wondering why we ran an additional RF line directly into the coaxial input of the HDTV (see photo #2). That was so we could use the PIP feature which allows you to watch two programs at once by using the tuner of the PVR plus the tuner of the HDTV itself. However, in my experience, PIP is kind of like sex—it's something you try a lot when everything is fresh and new, but over the years the frequency goes way down.

11) The final step is to buy a bigger coffee table. You'll need it for the remotes (see photo #4). The HDTV, PVR, DVD, VHS VCR and surround-sound RCVR all have their own remotes. I also suggest you buy a universal remote—not to use, just to have on hand as a place to store batteries.

Photo #4

You're now ready to go, so plug everything in and turn it on. Put a DVD in the DVD and a VHS in the VCR. Press PLAY on each of their remotes. The rest is easy. Turn on the PVR and set the channel to Discovery in hi-def. Even though you'll never watch Discovery, it's a great channel to test for beautiful pictures. Pick up the HDTV remote and turn the set on. Keep pressing the INPUT button until you've seen all of your signals show up. The sequence should go like this: basic cable (from the RF coaxial input), hi-def (Discovery from the PVR), DVD (from the DVD player) and crappy VHS (from the crappy VHS VCR). Now go back to the PVR and set it to your favourite show. Next, pick up the surround-sound RCVR remote and turn the audio up loud. How cool is that? Now sit back and enjoy your favourite program. And with the surround sound, you can almost hear what the wrestlers are thinking.

HOW TO HAVE A UFO SIGHTING

For anyone who enjoys science fiction, loves adventure or would just like to disprove every religion there ever was, there's something incredibly appealing about having your very own UFO sighting. It's not impossible, but it's also not easy. So if you're wondering if it could happen to you, here's a short list of some of the things you'll have to do to allow yourself to become one of the chosen few. Let's see if you've got the right stuff.

- Go to the highest hilltop in your area, away from the ambient light of the city, where you have a clear view of the night sky. While you're waiting for the sun to go down, eat every mushroom you can find.
- Live near an airport.
- When watching for UFOs, always remove your glasses.
- Convince yourself that there is superior intelligence on other planets and that it's only the stupid people on Earth who can't see their spaceships.
- Realize that you're a drab, boring person with no special skill or talent, but all of that will change the minute you see your first flying saucer.

- Learn how to take pictures while jiggling the camera so that the resultant image could be anything.
- Always watch for UFOs alone. No two people have ever seen the same UFO simultaneously, which proves that the aliens are so clever they only reveal themselves to us one at a time.
- Don't go on and on to your co-workers about the existence of UFOs. Just pretend you know something (it won't be easy).
- Exercise your imagination. Stare at clouds until they look like large-breasted women. Try squinting at things to make them look interesting. Like you do in the mirror.
- Use your diet. Many UFO sightings have occurred after a night of Indian food.
- Work on your credibility by pretending to have seen a UFO and watching people's reactions as you describe the experience. You will soon figure out how far you can go.
- Even after you see a UFO, be careful how you report it. Try to keep your language scientific and exact. Describing the shape as parabolic sounds way better than saying it looked like Elmer Fudd's ear.
- Don't embellish. The UFO sighting is enough. Don't add the part about how the aliens abducted you and took you bowling on Saturn.
- Don't assume a sighting is taking place. If people start yelling "UFO!" it might just be their way of telling you to leave.

THE EASY WAY TO RAISE CHILDREN

Raising children is not difficult, as anyone who doesn't have any will tell you. There is a lot of talk about managing your children and moulding them into productive adults, but that can be frustrating and extremely time-consuming. The key is to reject only the behaviour that you consider unpleasant or inconvenient. Yes, you are a parent, but you deserve to have at least as much fun as your kids do. Here are some quick easy ways to simplify rearing.

- Have a TV in every room.
- As soon as your child says his first word, get him a cell phone.
- Time is money. It's often better if you give your child money rather than time. If you don't have either, try giving them someone else's money. Bad money is better than quality time.
- Don't take them anywhere that has a dress code.
- Give them examples of people who had great lives but never really did anything—Rip Van Winkle, Boxcar Willie, Stéphane Dion, Jimmy Carter.
- Find a neighbour who really like kids and send yours over there.
- Kids love fast food, so why fight it? Make sure at least one meal a day comes through a car window.
- Don't be a pain about setting curfews. You can tell your kid that he needs to be home by midnight, but let him pick the time zone.
- Don't nitpick about whether or not he's attending school. If he's out of the house all day, that's good enough.
- Create special routines. Kids love family traditions. For example, buying lottery tickets.
- Teach your children to never confess. Admission of guilt is the first step towards taking personal responsibility—goodbye, happy life.
- Let him know that any behaviour is acceptable. If he gets a tattoo, YOU get a tattoo. If he gets his genitals pierced, YOU get a tattoo.

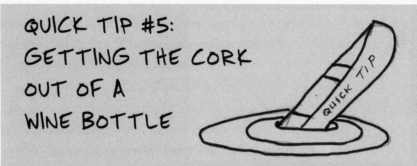

QUICK TIP #5: GETTING THE CORK OUT OF A WINE BOTTLE

Maybe you don't have a proper corkscrew, and maybe hammering a spiral nail into the cork and then trying to pull it out with a claw hammer didn't go so well. Well, here's what you do. Open the canister on your Shop-Vac and jam the wine bottle up into the hose opening. Close it up and shove a large apple or potato or any other turgid fruit into the end of the nozzle to stop the airflow. When you turn on the machine, you will create a vacuum around the bottle, causing the air pressure inside to blow the cork out. When you hear the cork hit the back of the turgid fruit, shut the unit off and enjoy.

HOW TO SELL A QUESTIONABLE USED CAR

It is human nature to want something for nothing, so no matter how little you're asking for your used car, the prospective buyer will be expecting a lot more quality than is reasonable. Unfortunately, this sad truth prevents you from being totally honest. While I'm not suggesting you lie, it is okay, and even necessary, to omit certain details and even imply certain untruths through ambiguous implication. The ultimate goal is to sell the vehicle; even at worst, the buyer learns enough to be able to sell the car to somebody else. Here are a few very acceptable tricks of the trade to help you unload that old stove you've been driving.

- If the engine is noisy, use additives. You can pour liquid honey or caramel pudding into the crankcase through the oil filler pipe. If it's still knocking, try chunks of fudge or small rubber dog toys.
- If lots of blue smoke is coming out of the exhaust pipe, jam a potato up in there. Just remember not to run the engine for long, and don't ever stand behind the car.
- If the odometer is reading over 300,000 klicks, get some beige nail polish or appliance enamel and put a small decimal point between the last two digits.
- If you have lots of power options, like power windows, keyless entry, power trunk lid, sunroof, etc., and none of them work, install a dead battery and blame everything on that.
- If one of the doors is missing, park the car in such a way that it's not noticeable. If two doors are missing, you may have a problem, unless they're both on the same side.
- If the car smells like smoke because it has been on fire a few times, avoid embarrassing questions by stuffing the ashtrays with cigarette butts.
- If the car just plain smells bad, put an onion in the glove compartment.
- Clean out the car. Most prospective buyers will be put off by any amount of manure in the back-seat area.
- If the tires are bald and you are an artistic type, you can draw tread on them with a fresh Sharpie.
- If you have a stone chip in the windshield (see the chapter on gravel driveways), hang large fuzzy dice to block the driver's view of the blemish.
- Imply that the car runs well by stuffing the console with unpaid speeding tickets.
- If the muffler is shot, turn up the radio.
- If the car has different coloured fenders and doors,

make sure it's dirty enough that you can't tell (probably not an issue).

HOW TO AVOID CONFLICT

It's usually better not to be in a fight than to win one. Even if you're bigger and stronger than your opponent, you may skin your knuckles on his glasses. I suggest you adjust your behaviour so that arguments don't escalate into fisticuffs. Here are a few tips to make this a kinder, gentler world.

- Don't say what you're thinking.
- Arrive home wearing the same clothes you left in.
- Never communicate directly with anyone in the tax department.
- Give the police one-word answers.
- Unless you're in Scotland, when the restroom door drawing is wearing a skirt, don't go in.
- When talking to an associate, don't say anything negative about his wife.
- When talking to an associate, don't say anything positive about his wife.
- Don't mess around with any animal that has bigger teeth than you.
- In any argument, the big guy with the chainsaw is always right.
- Don't eat food from a country that doesn't have houses.
- Don't insult your surgeon until after the operation.
- Never argue with anyone who can outrun you.
- Accept the premise that not one person in the judicial system has a sense of humour.

- When going through security, don't strip naked unless they ask you to.
- Anything you say to your wife will be held against you, even if her name is not Miranda.
- When you're at a family gathering, remember that secrets are often a good thing.
- If nobody's asking for your opinion, they're probably right.

THE IMPORTANCE OF A GROUND WIRE

Back in the old days, we all had television antennas up on our roofs. They were rendered obsolete by cable because nobody'd been able to figure out how to charge a hundred bucks a month for a TV aerial. Anyway, back then, every TV antenna had what was called a ground wire. It was a pretty heavy steel cable that went from the antenna into a peg driven a few feet into the ground. The purpose of the ground wire was to take electricity from lightning hitting the antenna and send it directly into the ground rather than letting it blow out through the TV, taking what was left of your hair with it. Even electric power tools always had that third wire to ground the machine so that, if you had a short, the electricity would go somewhere safe rather than into your arm or your lip or whatever body part you had straddling the instrument.

Well, nowadays, as I said earlier, we don't have TV antennas, so there's no ground wire there, and most power tools have even dispensed with them because they claim to have insulated the electrical parts from the tool housing. And maybe they have, when the device is brand new and still in the box. But once you've used it a couple of times and dropped it down a well or backed a tractor over it, chances are the housing isn't nearly as well insulated as everybody had hoped. And anyone who's ever been up a ladder with a Skilsaw can tell you that electricity will make you do things you never intended. Let's not forget that Earth is one of the harder planets—probably due to the gravity, which is another problem for the guy on the ladder.

The point I'm trying to make here is that we need to bring back the ground wire. Every man needs something in his life that will take the hit for him when things go wrong. It's not fair to expect your friends and family members to do it.

HOW TO FEEL GOOD ABOUT YOURSELF

- Sell all your mirrors.
- Learn how to use Adobe Photoshop to attach pictures of your head to attractive bodies—of the same gender (and species).
- Do NOT make a resumé.
- Stay away from reunions.
- When a friend arranges for a stranger to meet you at the airport, do not ask the stranger how the friend described you.
- Use the GUINNESS BOOK OF WORLD RECORDS to find people who are shorter, fatter, uglier and stupider than you.
- Don't look too far ahead, and don't look back at all.
- Work on identifying the positive aspects of your personality. If you can't think of any, that qualifies as humility. It's a start.
- Do something you're proud of. Failing that, stop doing something you're ashamed of.

WHAT TO DO WITH YOUR FITNESS EQUIPMENT

If you're like me, over the years you've probably gathered quite a selection of fitness equipment that is now covered with wet laundry or old paint cans or whatever, and you can't even sell it at a garage sale because garage sale customers have the same stuff at their homes. So what do you do? Well, in the military they call it redeployment. Here, we call it still being useless, but in a very innovative way.

Let's start simple. Position your stationary bike right beside your desk, then jam your letter paper, envelopes and greeting cards in between the spokes, and in a matter of minutes you've converted a stationary bike into a *stationery* bike.

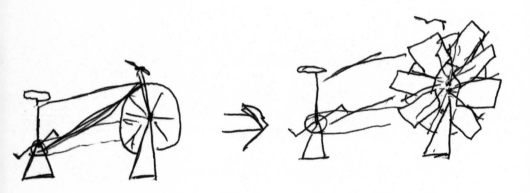

Let's move on to the treadmills. Yes, I said treadmills, plural. I know you and your wife have one each because you couldn't figure out how to change the settings. Remove the handrails with a ¾-inch socket wrench or a small car at moderate speed. Then mount the treadmill bases on top of your kitchen counter on either side of the sink. Place a garbage can on the floor at one end of the counter. All day, put your dirty dishes on one side and your garbage on the other. Before you go to bed, turn on the treadmills and watch your dishes go into the sink and your garbage go into the can while you go into the sack.

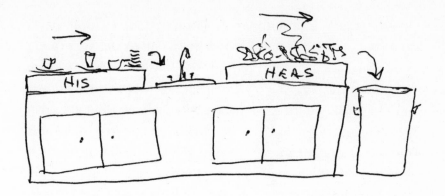

If you want to get even more creative with your treadmill, and you love art, take the base and mount it vertically on the wall behind an empty picture frame. Then take your collection of velvet paintings out of their frames and glue them onto the treadmill belt. Now you can just run the treadmill to find the exact painting that suits your mood on any particular day. Use your old sweatpants to hide the other pictures. They probably don't fit you anymore anyway.

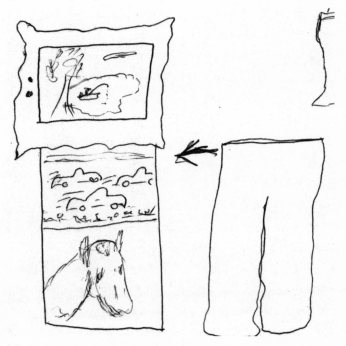

* Ignore that extra bit of drawing in the upper right-hand corner.

Now we get a little more complicated, so if you feel a headache coming on, you may want to skip to the next section. We're going to use your stair stepper as a retractable snack tray. As you know, with a stair stepper, when one step goes up the other goes down, and vice versa. So attach a racing-bike pedal to your favourite beer stein and put your snack bowl on the lower step of the unit. Pour a couple of beers into the stein. Pick it up with your foot and place it on the high step. The weight of the stein will force the snack bowl up. Have a few nibblies, and when you're ready to get back to serious drinking, pick up the stein with your foot again and the snack step will drop, taking the bowl out of sight so it doesn't block your view of the hockey game.

And now the pièce de résistance: keeping the toilet lid down so the dog doesn't drink out of it. It's important work, because this is the same dog that licks your face. And it's such an easy fix. Just a little duct tape and a Thighmaster and it's last call for Fido. The only change *you* have to make is to remember that relieving yourself is now a two-handed affair.

APPEARANCES CAN BE REVEALING

If you're observant, you can learn a lot about a person just from certain details in their appearance or behaviour. I'm not talking about profiling here, because I'm not allowed to. I mean little signs you can look for; after you see them, you'll immediately know a lot more about that person than they expected you to, because generally people assume you're an idiot.

Here are a few tips to help you delay that discovery.

- If the person has no eyebrows, they have recently purchased their first barbecue.
- If the person talks about suicide, they are a golfer.
- If the person has no cuts or scars on their right hand, they are left-handed.
- If the person asks you to turn the heat up, they are not wearing underwear.
- If the person has several welts and bruises on their forehead, they live in a basement apartment.
- If the person blinks and twitches a lot, they have recently been struck by lightning.
- If the person eats a lot of cheese, they have outdoor plumbing.
- If the person is itchy, they will steal one of your forks.
- If the person is boring, they are married.
- If the person has big teeth, they also have a big mouth.
- If the person is eating a raw onion, they will be leaving early and alone.
- If the person plays nervously with their car keys, they have a wife who likes to shop.
- If the person talks only about the future, they have been incarcerated.
- If the person doesn't listen to anyone, they're in politics.

HOW TO BABYSIT

No matter how hard you try to avoid it, the day is going to come when, for whatever reason, you have to look after a baby. There are a couple of important things you need to know before you take that on. First of all, it's vital that the baby in question is bottle-fed. That's a deal-breaker. Also, you'll be told that the baby naps a lot—well, so do you, so you really have no advantage there.

Here's another bulletin: babies cry. It's really their only way of communicating—like you, after seven beers. So don't get upset if the baby cries. Instead, try to figure out what's wrong. The baby may be hungry or wet, or hungry *and* wet, or may just need to be held. Babies like to be held, but not by the ankles. They need to feel that you're supporting and protecting them. Hold them in your arms snugly, but not firmly, and make sure the head's on top.

After feeding the baby, you will need to burp it—perhaps the first thing the two of you can do together. If you don't burp the baby, it will spit up. And that will happen while you're holding the baby—usually while you're holding the baby on your shoulder, so you won't know it spit up until you feel the dampness on the back of your leg.

Of course, your biggest fear is that the baby will need a diaper change. That fear will be realized. While it's not the most pleasant assignment you'll ever face, you need to put it in perspective. The laws of physics are on your side; whatever comes out of the baby will be smaller than the baby, so if you pick up the baby, you can surely pick up the satellite it throws off. And a good guideline to help you decide when to change a baby is to use the same rule you use on all your handyman projects: never clean up until the job is completely done.

HOW TO BALANCE YOUR BOOKS

Over the years, I've tried everything I could think of to keep my financial records in order, and nothing has really worked for me. Mind you, I started with no knowledge or interest, and since then I have lost even more. When I got my first bank account,

I thought that as long as I still had cheques left, I couldn't possibly be overdrawn. That was a mistake. Then, after I got my credit card, I was continually shocked by hidden charges and late payment penalties and by being billed even when I'd badly forged my own name. It was a mess. So now I have come up with a failsafe way to keep your finances in order. And I know it's idiot-proof because *I've* used it.

Step One: Get a small toolbox with a padlock on it.

Step Two: From the first to the fifteenth of each month, spend normally, by cash, cheque and credit card.

Step Three: On the sixteenth of the month, stop spending. Put your cash, your chequebook and your credit card into the toolbox. Lock the padlock and mail yourself the key.

Step Four: The postal system being what it is, the key won't arrive at your house until the end of the month. When it does, you are ready to balance your books.

Step Five: Open the padlock and remove your cash, chequebook and credit card. The two-week delay has allowed plenty of time for all of your cheques and charges to clear, so now simply phone the credit card company and ask for your current balance (call this number A). Now phone the bank and ask how much money is in your account (number B). If number B is greater than number A, pay off your credit card with a cheque and top up your cash position. If number B is less than number A but greater then the minimum payment, pay the minimum and try to catch up next month. If number B is even less than the minimum payment, lock the cheques, credit card and cash back up and give the key to your wife. When she returns it to you, you'll know that you're back in business.

HOW TO HANDLE MESSY PEOPLE

Before I get into this, I think we should define what I consider to be a messy person. I'm not one of those anal, neat-freak types who would rather never do anything than make a mess. The truth is, there are certain types of messes that are acceptable and certain types that aren't. If you look in my toolbox you'll find wrenches mixed in with screwdrivers and duct tape mixed in with everything, but the point is *they're all tools*. You won't find a pair of binoculars and a work sock in there. So I'm saying that a logical, rational mess is okay; a random, unclassified mess is not. If you live or work with somebody who looks at it the other way, you know how frustrating it can be. And if you don't, maybe *they* do. In any case, there are some things you can do that will eventually alter their behaviour.

The first step is to get to the core elements of the problem:

1) A messy person doesn't mind a mess. They've probably been messy for so long they don't even notice it.
2) They don't clean up because there's always something more pleasant or important for them to do.
3) When they finish with something, they either assume they're going to need it again soon, so they don't put it away, or they don't think they'll ever need it again, so they don't put it away.

You're not going to break that pattern through arguing or even using electroshock therapy. They'll tidy up when tidying up becomes their best personal choice. So instead of browbeating them, you need to step back and observe their behaviour for a week. Once you have a sense of their routines and patterns, you can start the treatment. Your objective is to make the person's mess an obstacle in their own lives rather than just an annoyance in yours. The preferred technique is to hide that person's personal items somewhere in their own mess. It can be their car keys buried in a pile of parking tickets, or a potentially winning lottery ticket down behind the filing cabinet, or their passport wedged deep into their chair, or their glasses in a potted plant. If they have a habit of leaving half-eaten snacks in their desk drawer, introduce mice into the environment. If you can get them to connect these problems to their own messiness, they will change.

Unless they're men.

QUICK TIP #6: FIXING A LEAKY ROOF

In the days of wooden ships, if there was a leak in the hull, the sailors would fill a box with sawdust, lower it to the general vicinity of the leak and pull the string that opened the lid. The water flowing through the hole in the hull would draw the sawdust into it and seal the leak. A garbage can full of sawdust dumped on your roof in the general area of the leak while it's raining will have the same results. One problem that you might have, that the sailors didn't, is wind. It's very rarely windy under water.

HOW TO INSTALL A PARQUET FLOOR

In case you don't know, parquet flooring goes way back in history. It's a bunch of small wooden tiles installed so the grains are at right angles, making an interesting pattern. (Parquet is pronounced "par-kay." In fact, if you want to spell it parkay, that's also oquet.)

The first step is to select the type of tile you want to use. There are a lot of different colours available. I recommend you go with a beer-coloured tile, because that's probably what you'll be spilling on it most often. Before you start, you must empty the room of all furniture. I know there's a temptation to save a few bucks by only tiling the open spots on the floor and not doing the areas under the couch and chairs, but you're not going to get a very tight fit—and if you're married, chances are the furniture will get moved around a lot, sometimes right out the door.

Once the room is empty, you need to measure the length and width and multiply those together, then divide by the area of a parquet tile. That will give you the number of tiles you need. If, the last time you did your own math, you ended up with thirty-seven extra rolls of non-returnable wallpaper, I suggest you just buy the tiles one box at a time until the floor is done.

Start by placing one tile in the centre of the room. If your room is a perfect square, this is going to be an easy job. Even if it's a rectangle, you'll be fine. But chances are it's a parallelogram—or worse yet, a random quadrilateral where none of the sides is parallel or even straight. So start in the centre and line up one edge of the tile with your favourite wall. A lot of tile manuals tell you to cut and lay the whole floor and then lift it all back up and redo the installation with glue. But depending on your level of patience and concern, and with an eye towards your life expectancy, you may not want to devote that kind of time to something you're going to walk on with dirty work boots. So I say just glue it down from the get-go. This glue is pretty toxic, so make sure you have plenty of ventilation. If you start humming Jefferson Airplane tunes, chances are you need to open another window.

Moving out from the centre tile, lay each one with the grain going at a ninety-degree angle to the next tile. When it's all done, the floor will look like the mowing pattern on the infield of Yankee Stadium. You'll find the job will go like halitosis—everything's fine until you get close. So as you approach the walls, you will notice that nothing is square and you will have some kind of bizarre extended triangular gap between the last row of tiles and the wall.

Now, if you're a purist, you can cut all the remaining tiles so that they fit snugly into each of the odd-shaped gaps. I suggest you just put extra glue on the last row so it won't move, then cover the gap with trim. You may find that the standard quarter round or other trims aren't wide enough to do the job, but if you go to a lumber salvage place you will find some old-style high baseboard trim from back in the days when a two-by-four was a two-by-four.

These old baseboards were meant to hug the wall and extend eight or nine inches up. For our purposes, we'll turn them ninety degrees so they hug the floor and extend eight or nine inches out. And you're done.

Don't let anybody see your work until you've put all the furniture in place. Maybe hang some pictures of good-looking scantily clad women to take the focus away from your flooring job. Hopefully you'll get some compliments, but if you really want them to swoon, leave the lid off the glue can.

THE MOTOR-SAIL-CLE

There's a lot of talk these days about wind power. It's coming from politicians, which adds credibility, since they know a lot about that particular subject. So here's an effective way to harness wind power by combining your knowledge of sailing with your love for motorcycles. I call it the motor-sail-cle, because I can.

Other than a motorcycle, the only thing you need is the mast and sail from a sailboat, which you can pick up very cheaply from any marina with inadequate security. Almost all of the overpasses on our highways have a maximum height of 13'6", so you'll need to trim the mast down to 13'5". Mount the mast and sail in such a way that when you're sitting on the motorcycle the boom can swing back and forth freely above your head. It is inconvenient to be knocked off a motorcycle at any speed above fifty klicks.

Once the sail is mounted, you're pretty much done. Head out on the highway and tailgate a transport truck. Try to pick one with large, clean brake lights so you get as much warning as possible about sudden stops. You will find a position about twelve feet behind the truck where the wind is constant as a result of the air being displaced by a vehicle of that size hurtling down the road. When you set the sail at the correct angle, you will be able to augment the power of the motorcycle engine with the tacking force of the wind. Under extreme conditions you may even be able to shift into neutral and let the sail do all the work, but that will require you to maintain balance by hiking way out to one side, which can be dangerous as you lose the ability to steer or stop. Still, the fuel savings make it all worthwhile. Give it a try, and best of luck.*

HOW TO TAKE BETTER PICTURES

There are good reasons why people very rarely look at pictures they've taken over the years. In some cases, they don't want to be reminded that they used to weigh less than two hundred pounds and had hair, but the main reason is that the pictures were crappy to begin with. To avoid future disappointment with your albums, simply take better pictures.

Also, I bet that when you give anyone a photo you've taken, they either throw it away or put it in a drawer for a while and then throw it away. One of the ways to prevent that happening is to frame the photo first, but a cheaper solution is, again, just to take better pictures. Here's how.

Use a camera. Not your phone. If your phone costs a hundred dollars, most of that is for the part that sends and receives calls. They didn't secretly hide a thousand-dollar camera in there.

Use a good digital camera. The resolution is indicated by the size of the photo file the camera creates. Twelve megabytes is going to give you very detailed pictures. Two hundred kilobytes is going to look like you drew the picture with a tube of lipstick.

See the light. Here's a shocker: when you look through the viewfinder, the brightest thing in the frame will be the brightest thing in the picture. So showing off Aunt Hazel's tan by having

---

* Only recommended in countries that have socialized medicine.

her stand between you and the sun will not give you the best results. Make sure the thing you want to highlight is the thing that's highly lit. That sure sounds like Aunt Hazel.

Put your glasses on. Even auto-focus can't correct for you failing to get Aunt Hazel in the frame—or including the guy in the background making that insensitive hand gesture.

Take fewer pictures. I know, it's the digital age and you can delete anything you don't like, but that shouldn't lower the bar. You're way better off to take one good picture than a hundred bad ones. I know a picture is worth a thousand words, but if it's a terrible picture most of those words will be obscenities.

Show people the picture from the camera monitor before you waste time and money printing it. Watch closely for their reaction. If anyone says, "What's that thing?" I suggest you delete the photo.

Know your subject. People with big egos want to be the focal point of a picture. Make sure you position them in such a way that their body is blocking anything that might otherwise be of interest. Conversely, people with low self-esteem or a high body-fat index need to be photographed inconspicuously. Have them stand beside (or behind) a giant sequoia.

No posers. Take natural pictures. Only the best professional photographers are capable of getting people to pose in a way that doesn't make them look like they've been immortalized by Madame Tussaud. Catch them smiling or laughing or even just staring off, wondering why they came to your party. There's an honesty in a natural photo that far outweighs the insult they may feel.

Know which subjects to avoid. No matter how well you light, frame and focus, there are certain things that will ruin any picture. It's generally a matter of using your common sense, but if that's not one of your strong suits, here's some subject matter to keep clear of: outhouses, drunks, pastel leisure suits, vomit, roadkill, septic trucks, animals fornicating, XXXL spandex, hairy-backed men, hairy-fronted women.

Do nothing. This is the best advice I can give. Take as many pictures as you want and then do nothing with them. Just leave them in the camera. If somebody wants one, great. You can print it off or, better still, email it to them and let them waste their own ink and ultra-premium glossy paper. If nobody wants one, that's also an important message. When you run out of space on the camera, delete the pictures that don't have you in them—and will the camera to a relative who has always ignored you.

YOUR FIRST CRUISE

It is difficult to survive middle age and marriage without at some point having to go on a cruise. I suggest you just bite the bullet and get it out of the way with a minimum of whining. Who knows, you might even enjoy it. At the very least, if it's a disaster, you don't want to be the one who made it that way.

The first step, before you even start packing, is to take a hard look at your suitcases. If they're old and frayed around the edges, with flower-power stickers covering the rips and holes, maybe it's time for an upgrade. They make them out of fibreglass now, so they're cheap and tough and it kind of feels like you're dragging a Corvette around. The quality of your luggage is important because the crew will be taking it off the bus and setting it in your cabin, and ratty luggage suggests you're cheap and low class, an impression you'd like to delay for as long as possible.

Now we get to the packing. The prime reason people take vacations with a ship full of strangers is so that they can overeat without their friends seeing them. So take your big clothes and your pants with elastic waistbands. Slip-on shoes are also handy for those last few days when you either can't bend over or can't see your feet.

You'll probably be a little shocked by how small your cabin is, and it will only get smaller as you expand. Plus, if you went on the cheap, you're probably in the lowest deck, at the back end of the ship, just a sheet of drywall away from the engine room. Look at the bright side: if the engine craps out, you'll be the first to know. As soon as you get settled into your cabin, they'll have a mandatory lifeboat drill. Just go quietly and keep your mouth shut. Telling *Titanic* jokes or faking a heart attack is not nearly as funny as you think.

Once you've been disciplined by a senior officer, the ship will leave port. You may notice that the ship pitches and sways a lot more than you expected. They'll tell you it's because they can't put the stabilizers down until they get farther out to sea. I'm not sure how they can assume six-foot waves without stabilizers will be rougher than twelve-foot waves *with* stabilizers, but as I mentioned above, you need to constantly remind yourself that you're not here to make trouble.

Okay, take a walk around the ship and look at all the stuff—the showrooms, the stores, the movie theatre, the casino, etc. There's lots to do, but don't be fooled. Your key to a cost-effective cruise is to sleep as often as possible. Here's the reasoning: the cruise line will serve seven meals daily. That's too much food for anybody to eat in one day, so rather than abstain and not get your money's worth, you need to turn each day into *two* days. And you do that by sleeping. Get up at 6 A.M., have breakfast, go to the gym and exercise your eyes, walk around the deck so nobody can talk to you, then have a big lunch at 10. Go to the top deck and hit golf balls into the ocean or stand at the prow of the ship and sing a medley of Céline Dion songs. Just be sure to keep your head tilted into the wind so that your comb-over doesn't whip around and smack you in the genitals. Then have a huge dinner at noon. Follow it with a nightcap, say good night and hit the sack. Get up around

2:30 for a midnight snack: an ice cream cone or dessert of some kind—cruise ships can make you eat anything by covering it in chocolate. Then go right back to sleep, because it's really the middle of the night for you. Set the alarm for 6 P.M. When it goes off, say good morning to your wife, have a shower and a shave and head over to the Lido deck for a hot breakfast. Followed by lunch at 8:30 P.M., then dinner at 11. You're back in bed by midnight, then up at 6 to start the cycle all over again. Suddenly, your four-day cruise just became an eight-day cruise for the same money. We're talking value. And it's even healthier, because your daily caloric intake is now half of the twenty-four-hour amount. It just makes good sense.

HOW TO SPLIT FIREWOOD

Any house that was built thirty or more years ago probably has some kind of wood-burning fireplace or wood stove or fireplace insert or something that everybody thought would save money and add a little something to the home's atmosphere without ruining the world's atmosphere.

While most homeowners have come to their senses and are either burning chemical logs or have switched to gas, there are still a handful of purists who get their own firewood with a chainsaw or a phone call and then are faced with the challenge of splitting the wood into a more manageable size. Many men who do this picture themselves as Paul Bunyan or at least Clint Walker, standing in the backyard with their shirts off while they use an axe to split firewood on a stump. As I've said for years, it is very dangerous for almost any man over forty to have his shirt off, even at rest. If he's actually doing something, the situation gets even worse. The centrifugal force of the axe swing sends pockets of fat into odd orbits around the navel, while the impact of hitting the log starts a ripple of jiggling that can last for most of a minute.

And the results are just as far from the dream. Instead of a clean, crisp crack, with the wood leaping into two almost identical halves, the axe lodges three inches in, and it's all you can do to pick it up with the weight of the log on the end. You slam it down weakly a couple of times on the stump, but that just jams it in harder. Next, you try standing on the log while rocking the axe handle back and forth to free it. You try wedging it under the deck for extra leverage. You might even drive over it with your car. Now you stand the log on the stump with the axe jammed in the top and you start hitting the axe head with a sledgehammer, driving it deep into the wood, but the log still doesn't split. And now the head is so far in you can't make contact, which you discover on your next swing, when the sledgehammer comes down and shears off the axe handle.

At this point, a lot of men buy a hydraulic wood splitter. You lay the wood into it, start the gas engine, pull the lever and apply a ton of pressure on the log. That's a lot of energy, and most of the time it splits the log. But when it doesn't, it splits the log splitter or the guy operating it. I suggest instead that you just leave the log out in the sun for a few years and eventually it will crack apart. Then you can get your axe head back. Keep it as a combination paperweight and reminder as to why we created central heat and high-efficiency furnaces in the first place.

At this point in your life, the best way to split firewood is to split *from* firewood.

COOKING WITH ACETYLENE

Often called "the handyman's microwave," an acetylene torch is a dandy way to cook meals when flavour takes a back seat to expediency. But as is true with so many potentially lethal tools, it's not a bad idea to figure out how they work first. The flame on an acetylene torch is around 1,200 degrees Fahrenheit, and cooking with that kind of heat can be like toasting marshmallows on the sun. The trick is to have a device that will constantly regulate the distance between the flame and the meal. The temperature goes down an average of a hundred degrees for every half-inch you move away from the flame. (If you need to have those numbers in metric, go ahead.) So if you want to cook a rump roast at 400 degrees, you'll need to keep it a consistent four inches from the flame. And as you'll see below, that's a lot easier than it sounds. The first step is to determine what category the food fits into:

a) Flat Things (steak, chops, fish, bacon, etc.), or
b) Round Things (roasts, turkey, ham, sausage, wieners, kielbasa, etc.).

Let's start with a flat thing, like a steak. The first step is to mount the acetylene torch on the needle arm of a lie detector. Lay the steak on the paper that scrolls through during a lie detector test. Next, light the torch, hook yourself up to the lie detector and phone the government to explain your tax return. The scrolling paper will move the steak under the flame, and your explanation will cause the torch to swing wildly and cook the whole surface of the steak. Flip the steak over and do another pass. If you don't want to talk to the tax department, try telling your wife why you came home late without calling. The more well-done you like your steak, the closer you should mount the torch to the meat. Or you could just do a lot more passes, which will require a lot more lies. You may have to bring in a stockbroker.

Round things are a little trickier. Let's say you want to do a baked potato. You need to get two identical potatoes, a lathe and a key-cutter jig. Put both potatoes end to end on the shaft of the lathe. Mount the torch on one end of the key-cutter jig. Set the guide arm of the jig to rub against the first potato while

OVERHEAD VIEW

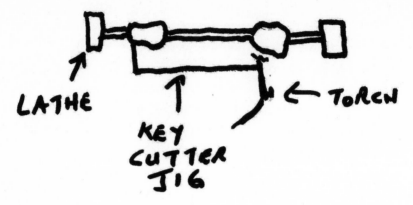

LATHE

KEY CUTTER JIG

← TORCH

the torch cooks the second one. As the lathe turns and the jig moves laterally, the torch will move in a pattern that mirrors the shape of the potato, thereby keeping the distance from the flame constant.

If you're on a limited budget and can't afford the cost or ridicule that come from cooking with shop tools, you could just cut your food into tiny pieces and hold them one at a time in the acetylene flame. A word of caution: let the food cool down before you eat it, and use an asbestos fork.

GETTING MORE OUT OF YOUR FURNACE

The three main components in your central-heating forced-air furnace are:

- the heat exchanger, which is a rectangular sheet-metal box that sits over top of the burner;
- the distribution fan, which pulls air in through the cold-air returns in the bottom of the walls, down through the heat exchanger to warm it, and then out through . . .

- the duct work, which brings the heated air through the floor vents into each of the rooms.

And though you may not realize it, there's a lot that your multi-featured, multi-talented furnace can do to improve your quality of life.

It can be turned into a home music centre. Switch off the burner. Open the access panel on the side of the heat exchanger and insert your boom box, pumping out your tunes. Turn on the distribution fan to send the music to every room in the house, and use the slides on each vent as individual volume controls.

It can deodorize your home. Remove the covers from the cold-air returns and fill them with lilac bushes. Turn on the distribution fan and your house smells like the botanical gardens rather than the compost heap.

It can safely expel propane gas. Propane is heavier than air, so if you have an accidental propane spill anywhere in the house, just reverse the polarity on the distribution fan so that the blades turn the other way, and the floor vents will become vacuums sucking the propane out of the room and into the furnace so that the resultant explosion happens well away from your furnishings.

It can cook your dinner. Again, take the side panel off the heat exchanger box and slide in a large pot of chili. Turn up the heat and enjoy the aroma wafting through the house as the dinner bubbles and boils. You can even use the furnace timer on the thermostat to stop cooking when you think the meal, and your guests, have all had enough—an excellent solution when chili night is a chilly night.

It makes you a member of the Forced Air Golf and Country Club. In the summer months, when the furnace is turned off, you can turn it into a putting practice facility.

Go to the driving range and start hitting balls with your normal swing and, while the attendant is ducking, take off with a small bucket of balls. Put the balls in your golf bag and leave the empty bucket in front of, and just below, the panel on the heat exchanger that you've removed yet again. Now adapt your floor vents so that they each have a golf hole in the middle of them. When you putt the ball into the hole, it will roll down through the duct work and drop into the bucket. If you have a big enough house, you may have enough vents for a full eighteen-hole course. Staircases make excellent elevated doglegs. (I'm sure you've seen your dog on the staircase with his leg elevated.)

HOW TO GET BACK AT YOUR LAWN MOWER

When your gas lawn mower finally gives out, the normal response is to just take it to the landfill or dump it in your neighbour's vegetable garden. But for me, that's not good enough. This is a machine that owes me. When I think of the number of times I had to swear at it or kick it, or the times I threw my back out trying to start it, I realize it does not deserve a decent burial. It needs to be punished for all of eternity.

You'll notice the engine head has cooling fins cast into it. Remove the head and mount it on the top step of your back porch. That's now for scraping the mud off your boots. Try it; it feels real good. Take out the piston and mount it on the floor as a doorstop. Then slam the door open into it as often as you want. Remove the pull cord from the starter and use it to carry the load of the counterweights for your garage door. Prop the garage door half open and let the weight just swing in the wind for an hour or two. Use the blade as a back-scratcher while you're watching the counterweight dangling there. Take out the spark plug and drop it into the septic tank. It won't do anything, but just knowing it's there will make you smile.

The next time you have a bonfire, hold a little ceremony, propose a little good-riddance toast and then, from a distance, lob the lawn mower's gas tank into the middle of the coals. Take the lawn mower handle and tie one of its arms to your bumper and the other to your buddy's bumper. Then, both of you drive away. Whichever of you ends up with the biggest piece gets to make a wish.

And for the final revenge, take all the remaining lawn mower parts and hang them in tiny nooses from the roof so they can watch you pave the lawn.

HOW TO SELL YOUR HOME PRIVATELY

With the current real estate slump and money being tight, most people are looking for new ways to maximize financial return. One of those ways is to avoid having to pay a commission by selling your home privately. As with most things in life, there's a right way and a wrong way to do that, and most of us have an almost uncanny ability to pick the latter. So to help you out, here are a few tips to make things go more smoothly.

1) Before you try to sell your house, it's important that you own it. Renting or leasing or knowing the real owner lives a long ways away is not good enough. The purchaser will search the title and won't see your name on it, and the whole deal will go sour. That's why they have FOR SALE BY OWNER signs rather than FOR SALE BY OCCUPANT. As a rule, you can't sell anything you don't own—unless you're a government or a mining company.

2) Identify the good points about the home and make sure you emphasize those. If it's a dump with a big yard, try to

avoid taking the buyer inside until absolutely necessary. If the morning sun shows the house off well, book the appointment for then. Same thing if the afternoon works better. If the house never looks good, show it at midnight.

3) Downplay the bad aspects of the house. If you're not sure what they are, take a few customers through it and watch for them to start jingling their car keys. Whatever you showed them just before that is what turned them off.

4) Pretend that it's killing you to sell this house. Make them think there's been some kind of financial reversal or job relocation or impending prison sentence that's forcing you to put the home on the market. Their sympathy will be overpowered by their misplaced sense of opportunity.

5) Don't say too much. Asides like "We hardly ever get a skunk in the basement" or "That huge pile of firewood will get you to Christmas," which may seem like brilliant value-adds to you, may discourage a prospective buyer with different tastes. In the Bible it says David killed thousands of Philistines with the jawbone of an ass. Many sales have been killed with the same weapon.

6) Don't bluff. If you get an offer, find a way to take it. Don't let your ego get in the way of your common sense. There may be certain conditions under which the buyer will pay more, but there are also many conditions under which you'll take less. Call it even and move on. If you get an offer, find a way to make it work. They say there's a customer for every home. But they don't say there are two of them.

Quick Tip #7:
HOW TO MEASURE YOUR HAT SIZE WITH A TWO-BY-FOUR

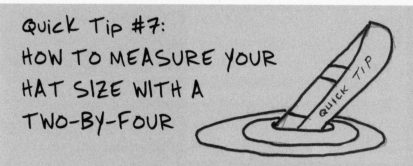

Chew four ropes of black licorice along with two packs of Dubble Bubble for about fifteen minutes. Take the gum-licorice combo out of your mouth and stick it on your forehead, either between your eyebrows or above your unibrow. The gum provides the stick-iness, the licorice provides the ink. Press a two-by-four against the glob, then roll the board round your head until it presses up against the glob a second time. Lay the two-by-four down and measure the distance between the licorice marks. Apply the measurement to the table below to get your hat size.

Head Size		Hat Size
Inches	Cm.	
21	53	6 ⅝
21 ½	54	6 ¾
21 ⅝	55	6 ⅞
22 ⅛	56	7
22 ½	57	7 ⅛
23	58	7 ¼
23 ⅜	59	7 ⅜
23 ¾	60	7 ½
24	61	7 ⅝
24 ½	62	7 ¾
25	63	7 ⅞

Let your hamster chew the glob off your forehead. Then go get that ermine fedora you've always wanted.

HOW TO SAVE MONEY ON AUTO BODY WORK

Recycle, reuse, renew, relax. That's how to save money in today's difficult economic times. And it even applies to doing auto body repairs. Maybe you've finally hit one too many fire hydrants or have ignored one too many speed bumps. Or maybe the road salt has finally eaten its way through your paint job, even though the paint is floor enamel and you put it on with a roller. Well, instead of going to an expensive body shop and making the vehicle look way better than it runs, why not use a little elbow grease and imagination to do those repairs right in your own garage?

First of all, examine the damage and put it into one of the following categories:

Dents. The word *dent* is short for "indentation." Dents go in. There's no metal missing, it's just that something that's supposed to be smooth and contiguous is now rough and not contiguous. The simplest solution is a toilet plunger. Coat the lip of the plunger with Vaseline, but don't let any of the neighbours see you doing that. Rumours are hurtful and spread quickly, particularly if Vaseline is involved. Once coated, apply the plunger to the middle of the dent, press in with all your might, then slowly pull the plunger out. Chances are the dent will pop right out. This brings us to the most important step: REMOVE THE PLUNGER. Driving around with a plunger sticking out the side of your vehicle gets the rumours going again and is just plain dangerous to hitchhikers.

Scratches. A scratch is an area where paint is missing. If you study a scratch through a microscope, you'll see it looks like your uncle's appendicitis scar. Something is missing, and you must replace the missing material to bring the car back to normal. If it's a really, really thin scratch that is only as deep as the final coat of paint, you can probably just paint over it with a small bottle of colour-matched auto paint and a tiny brush made from your own nose hairs. If the scratch is deep enough to go through all the layers of paint and undercoating and even into the metal, you need to fill that crevice up with chewing gum or cheese or overcooked pasta. Then, once it dries, you can paint it using the aforementioned nose-hair brush.

Holes. Holes represent pieces of metal that have gone missing because they rusted out or were punctured with sharp objects or were bludgeoned with a blunt instrument. The problem here is that you have to find a material that can bridge the gap. Depending on the size of the chasm, you could use pieces of newspaper soaked in varnish, or a pair of work socks dipped in epoxy, or even a section of screen. Once you've filled the hole—or holes—apply a coat or two of house plaster over the top, although this is not recommended if your roads have a lot of potholes. Plaster was never intended to withstand the jarring impact of an automobile going through a pothole at speed. For that, you need drywall.

Missing body parts. The absence of body parts is a most serious problem, as auto body shops charge you an arm and a leg. A fender can easily be a thousand dollars but you don't need the actual fender, you just need something that more or less has the same shape as the fender. You could even replace a metal fender with something that will last longer—like, say, a plastic garbage can. If you can use a little imagination and are good with snips, you can convert lots of existing household products into car body parts—a plastic flying saucer toboggan, a five-gallon gas can, a vinyl laundry hamper or a polypropylene dock box. Just cut out the part that you need, duct tape it in place, plaster the seams, fill any scratches with gum as described above and then paint it with your nose-hair brush.

Finish the job. Once you've completed all of the above, you must immediately get rid of the vehicle. See "How to Sell a Questionable Used Car" somewhere else in this book.

HOW TO USE AN ADJUSTABLE WRENCH

About the only thing duct tape can't do is take things apart. For that, you can either have a six-by-four-foot tool chest with five hundred wrenches varying in size from $1/32$" to two feet, or you can have one adjustable wrench. But, of course, all that means nothing if you don't know how to use it.

AS A WRENCH

Open the jaws by turning the cute little auger in a clockwise direction—or left to right, depending on whether you have the wrench out in front of you or are straddling it. Now place the jaws around whatever you're trying to undo and tighten them up by turning the auger the other way. Once they're snug, slide the wrench off and tighten it another smidge. This will make the wrench a little hard to get back on the nut, but it will be worth it. Now you can horse on the handle until the nut starts to turn. If you need more leverage, you can slide a piece of pipe over the end of the wrench, but don't exceed the manufacturer's warning that you will void the warranty if you use a pipe that is more than ten times the length of the adjustable wrench.

AS A HAMMER

Close the jaws tightly. We've all seen people flailing away at a pipe or an engine block with an adjustable wrench with the jaws wide open. This to me is the sign of an amateur handyman who has no respect for his tools. Close the jaws tightly and, with a firm grip in the strongest of your hands, make large, sweeping arcs with the wrench until it comes in contact with the target. Clear an area under the target so you have room to start the swing with the lower body; this will greatly increase the torque and your WHS (wrench head speed).

AS A PRY BAR

Slip the handle of the wrench under whatever it is you're trying to pry, then open the jaws up so they are slightly narrower than your heel. Now stand on the jaws. If that's not enough leverage, use a fireplace poker. You'll need the one with the crossbar a few inches from the end. Set the wrench jaws wide enough to take the poker, but narrower than the crossbar. Insert the poker as shown and push down where the arrows indicate. If your family has a circus background, you could even try standing on the poker handle.

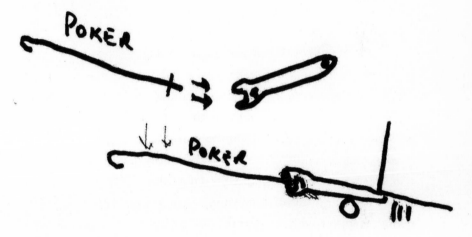

AS A CHAIN EXTENDER

Sometimes when you're trying to pull your snowmobile out of the lake, the tow chain needs just another few inches to reach the runner pin, and you can't back up your vehicle because the floorboards are already under water. So slip the handle of the adjustable wrench through the last link as shown. The width of the jaws will prevent it from slipping all the way through; then, just slip the hole in the wrench handle over the pin and haul away. If you're going to tow the snowmobile for a mile or more,

I suggest you wrap both ends of the wrench with the Handyman's Secret Weapon.

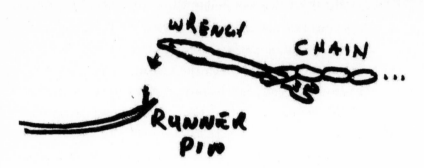

THE BENEFITS OF FISHING

People who don't fish can't understand why anybody would spend that kind of money flying in to some remote wilderness lake just to get up early in the morning and spend all day in a boat with a couple of other guys with no real guarantee that you'll catch anything—and even if you do, the cost of the fish works out to around five hundred dollars a pound. Well, those people feel that way because they don't understand the benefits of fishing. The actual catching of fish, while enjoyable, is merely a minor perk. Here are a few of the bigger ones.

Confidentiality. Nothing that you say or hear will be used against you, because everybody else is just as dumb and insensitive as you are. Nobody's going to rat you out because if you lose a guy, that's one less person to share the cost of next year's trip.

Privacy. Nobody outside of your small circle of friends has any idea what you're saying or doing. And if your friends are men, they're not paying attention, either.

Simplicity. Fishing does not call for multi-tasking. You only have one thing to do all day, and if you screw it up, it doesn't even matter.

Peace. Fishing is a serene activity. The only confrontation is between your lure and the fish, and even when that happens, it's under water, so you can't hear it.

Instant gratification. You catch a fish, you measure it, you clean it, you eat it. No reporting, no employee evaluation, no review board, no waiting for outside approval. You are the man.

Limited communication. It's a nice break to be with people who don't want you to talk. They say that conversation scares the fish away, but mainly conversation irritates the other fishermen. Short bursts of jokes or opinions are fine, but it's the long periods of silence that keep everybody coming back.

Acceptance. No matter how you look, chances are the guy in the rubber pants and plaid shirt with the fish hooks jammed into his THIS END UP ball cap is not going to judge you.

Fulfillment. There's something primal about going out into the wilderness with nothing but a line and a pole and a three-thousand-dollar fish finder, and coming home with dinner. Even if you don't catch anything, when you find out about the lives of the other guys, you'll probably feel better about your own.

Achievability. We're talking about four unshaven guys who will eat and drink anything, spending the weekend together with a vague hope of catching some fish. You can do this. You are not a loser.

Trust. There is an unspoken understanding among the group that this is something you plan to do every year, with the same people, until you are no longer physically capable of getting into a small plane or writing a big cheque.

WAKE-UP CALLS

It's surprising that many of the things our teachers and parents warned us about have turned out to be correct. Think of all the behaviour patterns, skills and attitudes they said we'd need to have to live happy and productive lives. And yet we ignored them and went our own way and now must pay the price. So here, in the interest of helping the next generation, are the warnings of past instructors and guardians of mine. It's too late for me, but maybe through my failure, the young people may find success.

- Punctuality doesn't seem important until you're late for your court appearance.
- You won't care about penmanship until you're trying to read your handwritten directions to the beer store.
- Personal hygiene becomes a priority when you're with four fat guys in a non-air-conditioned van.
- Math becomes useful when you're subtracting your height from the length of rope for the bungee jump.
- Spelling counts when you're making a sign that reads FRAT HOUSE.
- Learn new words every day. Lying is much more convincing when you have a large vocabulary.
- Reading comprehension is critical when consulting the instructions for the home enema kit.
- You should wear clean underpants. You may never be in an accident, but the underpants might.
- You're going to wish you'd learned about acids and bases when you wash off your car battery with laundry detergent.
- If you understood Newton's Laws of Physics, you would never have straddled that two-by-four.
- An appreciation of Geography can prevent you from becoming History.

- Knowing other languages comes in handy when you need to swear without getting caught.
- Maybe if you paid a little more attention to Botany, you wouldn't be lying awake scratching yourself right now.

HOW TO AVOID IDENTITY THEFT

We hear a lot of talk these days about identity theft. Somebody pretends to be you so they can use your credit cards or tap into your bank accounts or generally use your good name to their personal advantage. To analyze identity theft, you need to compare it to auto theft. The more appealing your car is, the more likely it will be stolen. Nobody ever boosts a Yugo. So the first solution to identity theft is to have an identity that's not worth stealing. It's easy to do. Withdraw all your money from the bank and max out your credit cards and you're there. If that's not your style, start spreading rumours about yourself, saying you're an undesirable person with links to organized crime.

Failing that—and this is big—do nothing. The truth is, identity theft is not really your problem; it's the bank's problem or the credit card company's problem. It's up to them to catch the crooks; it's not up to you to prevent crooks from existing. Back in the old days, when somebody forged a cheque, they didn't call it identity theft. It was called a forged cheque. And if the cheque cleared, it was because somebody at the bank didn't compare the signature or didn't ask for identification. But they took responsibility. They didn't try to blame us for their mistake. They created this banking system where they would hold your money and invest it and pay you about one-tenth of what they were making on your money, but the trade-off is you'd be allowed to access your own money easily through these things called cheques, which were really your own personal currency.

And the unspoken part of the agreement was that they were guaranteeing that your money would be safe. Some crook being allowed to cash a forged cheque on your account is no different than a bank robbery.

When you see the movies where the bad guys are stealing money out of the vault, that's not the bank's money, that's people's money. But the bank always took responsibility. They called it insurance. So now they've built this industry of credit cards and it's built on trust and they know that and once they lose that trust, nobody's going to use credit cards anymore. So the security of the system becomes a top priority. But by calling it "identity theft," they make us all feel like somehow we were lax and, when we weren't looking, somebody stole our souls. Whereas if we give it the right name, which is credit card fraud or cheque forgery, the responsibility goes back to the financial institutions who sold us the service in the first place. So I say they need to change their approach just a bit and admit they have a vulnerability in this area and they know it's their responsibility, but the truth is it affects everyone, so if we would please help them, we'd also be helping ourselves. I think we'd all be there in a flash. And it would feel so good to realize it's not our fault.

HOW TO FIGHT THE AGING PROCESS

I have very simple advice when it comes to fighting the aging process: don't.

Now, don't get me wrong. I'm not suggesting you should just let yourself deteriorate beyond any sense of decency, and I know it's good to have youthful attitudes, but I'm talking about society's preoccupation with trying to look twenty years younger than we really are. Hair dyes and facelifts and tummy tucks and personal trainers and every way possible to reverse the aging process by paying somebody to hurt you. I say go the other way. Try to look older than you really are.

Here's why: if you're fifty-five, it's not enough to just *look* thirty-five, you have to *think*—and more importantly, *act*—thirty-five. That will require you to drop all of your old-guy attitudes and pitch in on moving day. That may be okay for the age you *look*, but it's not okay for the age you *are*.

Let's say you have three guys, all fifty-five years old. One guy has bought the whole Hollywood package. He works out, he dyes his transplanted hair, he's had so many facelifts that most of his life is tucked behind his ears. He looks thirty-five. He gets lots of compliments. He can't wait to tell people how old he is. He has no friends and an unhappy wife. Guys his age aren't comfortable around him. They see his commitment to being young as an insult and a betrayal. His wife, similarly, feels incredible pressure not to look like his mother. And he doesn't do any better with thirty-five-year-old guys, with his Beach Boys cassettes and theories on Reaganomics. More than a fish out of water, he's like a flying fish in a bird sanctuary.

Now, the second guy looks fifty-five. He's had a normal life and takes reasonably good care of himself but lets nature pretty much decide what happens to his looks. So he's balding, with a lot of grey hair and all the wrinkles that befit a man a half-century into the game. He's got tons of friends his age, and his wife tolerates him and they look acceptable together—and once you're in your fifties, that's as close to love as you get. So this guy is fine. He may not be a millionaire, but he's at least got all the money the first guy spent on hair and tight skin.

Now we go to my personal hero, the third guy. He's also fifty-five but he looks about eighty. He needs a haircut. He's got bags under his eyes. On the rare occasion when he gets off the couch, he moves slowly. He needs ten minutes' warning when planning a trip to the restroom. His vital organs are in good shape, but everything else looks like he got it at the thrift store. He's my hero because he makes everybody around him feel good. Guys his age look younger when they're with him. His wife is often mistaken for his daughter, which is never a bad thing. And the benefit for him is that he's never asked to do any heavy lifting—or, in fact, anything. People think it's a miracle that he's even alive. I don't see a downside.

So I suggest you have a long talk with your vanity and then start focusing on your reality. Thirty-five is for thirty-five-year-olds. Stop trying to reverse time; hit the fast-forward button.

GOOD IN THE CLUTCH

Back in the early days of the automobile, there was no such thing as an automatic transmission. You had a clutch and you had a gearshift. Sometimes, the shifter was on the floor, as in "four on the floor," and sometimes it was on the steering column, as in "three on the tree." The Nash Metropolitan was so small, they had to put the gearshift on the dashboard. These days, manual transmissions are pretty much limited to trucks and sports cars. This is a huge mistake. There are so many pluses to a manual transmission that I think it's time to go back and revisit a good idea from the past. Here are just a few of the advantages to changing your own gears.

- You're the boss. You have much more control over how much gas you burn and how much power you use, based on controlling the revs of the motor through deciding what gear you should be in.
- Dead battery? No problem. Just put her in second gear, turn the key on, a couple of buddies can give you a quick push start and you're on your way. Can't do that with any stinking automatic.
- Brakes nearly shot? No worries. Use the gears to slow

yourself down and then clamp on the binders for the last few feet.

- Getting annoyed with drivers holding cell phones up to their ears? Never happens with manual transmission. When you've got both hands and both feet working, there are no appendages left to take that call. Gotta go hands-free or better yet, turn the cell phone off, which will take yourself and every other driver off the hook.

- Less maintenance. A car with manual transmission is a much simpler machine than its automatic counterpart. The automatic uses special fluid running through hydraulic pumps and controlled by servos that are triggered by the power demands and rpm's of the engine. You're replacing all of that technical intricacy with your left leg. An average transmission repair costs a thousand dollars. An average left-leg repair is covered by your health insurance.

- Fitness component. How ironic that people today drive their automatic cars over to the fitness centre so they can exercise their leg muscles. With manual, you just throw on a heavy-duty clutch spring, and every traffic jam is like doing fifty squats. And it's free.

- Hanky-panky proof. Just like the cell phone example, when you've got both hands and legs occupied, there's far less chance of any shenanigans going on as you and your heartthrob are motoring along our highways and byways. Mind you, the advantages all evaporate as soon as you park. It's like a bad case of gas—you're only safe as long as you keep moving.

STARTING YOUR CHAINSAW

You finally have a free Saturday and all you can think is that a tree is just a campfire waiting to happen. Or, at the very least, that you can finally clean up the scrub trees and brush that are blocking the neighbour's view of the inverted rusty van in your backyard. The only problem is that you can't get the darn chainsaw to start. Maybe the following will help.

Chainsaw motors are small and light with virtually zero torque, so they have to generate horsepower through extremely high rpm's. Because they're two-cycle engines, they can rev high without the added chore of opening and closing valves. The problem with two-cycle motors is that they burn oil, which tends to foul the spark plug. (That's another issue: one cylinder, one spark plug—if it doesn't fire, there's no help from anywhere else.)

The challenge is compounded by the fact that chainsaws are pull-starters. Whether you slide your foot through the handle and pull straight up, or drop the saw with one hand while you pull on the cord with the other, at some point you have a much better chance of starting your own bursitis than you do of starting your chainsaw.

Chainsaws have a choke control. Ideally, these help a cold chainsaw start by enriching the fuel mixture. In practice, if you have the choke on and the chainsaw won't start, the mixture is too rich. If you have the choke off and the chainsaw won't start, it's too lean. The choke is a lot like being married—it gives you several new ways to be wrong.

It's always a good place to start by removing and cleaning or replacing the spark plug. It can usually be cleaned and regapped, but if it comes out looking like a wet charcoal briquet, it's time for a new plug. Before reinstalling, hook up the spark plug wire and lay the plug on the engine casing while you gently pull the starter cord. You should see a spark. If you're not sure, sit on the plug while you pull the cord. That should give *you* a start.

If your chainsaw is a bit older, it may have low compression and you'll need to increase the rotation speed before it will start. That will take some decent arm strength, but if you don't have a teenaged son, you need to look at other options. You can add an extra twenty feet to the pull cord so that you can get a run at it or even tie it to your truck bumper. Or you can take the cutting chain off and instead run the chain from your stationary bike around the engine sprocket (see diagram). Although effective, there are a couple of problems with this technique. When the chainsaw starts, you need to take your feet off the pedals immediately. And under no circumstance should you attempt to put the cutting chain back on the machine while it's running.

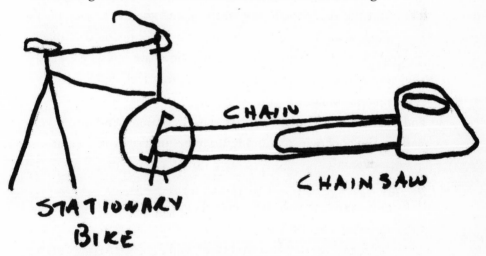

CHAIN

CHAINSAW

STATIONARY
BIKE

If you try all of the above and the chainsaw still doesn't start, try placing a ten-pound sledgehammer on the engine block—at speed, and repeatedly. It still won't start, but you'll feel better.

HOW TO AVOID TRAFFIC VIOLATIONS

Of all the unexpected situations in life, there's none more annoying or embarrassing than being pulled over for a traffic violation.* So it would probably be a good thing if I could help you avoid such things. I have years of experience in this area. As always, before you can even start to come up with a solution, you must first identify the fundamental elements of the problem. They are:

1) There are traffic laws and they will be enforced.
2) The police department expects to earn revenue from traffic violations.
3) Every citizen wants traffic violators to be caught and fined, unless it's them.

The result of these tenets is that if you get a ticket in a town of ten thousand people, one will fight it and the other 9,999 will sit quietly. The solution is to not get the ticket in the first place. To do that, you need to understand the basic laws of logic as they pertain to traffic violations. They are:

1) One policeman can only deal with one perp at a time.
2) Given the choice, the cop will always pull over the worst offender

This means there are only two ways to avoid getting pulled over for a traffic violation:

1) Don't break the traffic laws.
2) Don't break the traffic laws as badly as the other guy does.

Let's focus on number two. Whenever you're driving anywhere, you need to scan the road for people going in the same general direction as you, then pick out at least one really offensive driver who has no respect for anybody else on the road. Thankfully, it's not hard to do. But even when you find that driver, your job is

---

* An open fly during your valedictory speech is a close second.

not over. You must also find another equally disrespectful driver. Your challenge now is to manoeuvre your car in such a way that you are always between these two offensive drivers. That way, no matter where the cops are, you're second banana and will be ignored. The only possible exception is at red lights, as it is possible that the first guy gets through and you don't. Your option there is to stop on the yellow and then the bad driver behind will rear-end you—which, although inconvenient, can be very profitable and is therefore a chance worth taking.

There's an adage in sports that whoever comes in second is the first loser, but in terms of traffic violations, whoever is just ahead of the guy who gets caught is the first winner. And everybody loves a winner.

QUICK TIP #8: GETTING RID OF A BAD SMELL

If you have a basement—or perhaps a home—that smells really bad, generously apply underarm deodorant to your upper lip.

HOW TO SURVIVE THE AIRPORT EXPERIENCE

No matter how much you whine or how many illnesses you can fake, at some point you are probably going to have go somewhere by airplane. If you haven't done it in a while, be warned: things have changed. So here are a few helpful suggestions to get you on your way with as few outbursts of uncontrolled rage as possible.

- Buy a ticket in advance. This is not a train or a bus. You can't just step up to the wicket and assume that they'll have a seat for you. No matter how much they want you to leave.
- Bring proper identification. That means your passport. Not your driver's licence or birth certificate or membership card for the Jelly of the Month Club.
- Unless you're travelling with someone under twelve years of age, don't use the automatic check-in computer because you won't have a clue how it works. If you try, it will just lead to frustration and eventual kicking of the machine and next thing you know, you're not on a plane but in a police car. Go to the counter and check in the old-fashioned way—with a human being.
- Don't bring much stuff. If you have two bags, they'll charge you. If your bag is overweight, they'll charge you. If your bag clashes with the airline logo, they'll charge you. It's cheaper to travel extra light and buy clothes when you get there.
- Once you have your boarding pass, stick it inside your passport and tuck the whole bundle into your safest pocket. If you lose either your passport or your boarding pass, life as you know it will be over.
- While you're standing in line, there are certain words you should not say: bomb, hijack, sabotage, suicide mission, or anything LIKE suicide mission—i.e., "airplane food."
- If you have carry-on luggage, make sure none of the following are in it: firearms, fireworks, fire starters—in short, anything with the word FIRE as a key

component. You also can't carry things like pocket knives or nasal scissors because the authorities are concerned you'll rush the cockpit and begin trimming the captain's nose hairs until you get what you want. Security guards are trained to look for all levels of potentially dangerous substances—guns and gun powder are on the lowest level, next up are plastic explosives and nitroglycerine, and on the highest level of danger is a normal-sized tube of toothpaste.

- IMPORTANT NOTE: You are going to have to take your shoes off. Don't make that an unpleasant experience for everyone else at the airport, even if it means rescheduling bath night.

- Once you've shown your passport and boarding pass and put your carry-on bag on the conveyor belt, it's time for you to go through the metal detector. Take a moment and think about this. It's called a metal detector for a reason. It will find your lucky money clip, no matter how deeply you stuff it down into your underwear. Save yourself the embarrassment. Take out all your coins and car keys and military medals that you bought on eBay and put them into the little dish. If you have a belt buckle with a full-sized motorcycle on it, take it off. If you're an old guy who wears his pants really high, wear flannel jogging pants. That's because on your trousers, your fly may be long enough to trigger the sensor.

- After you get through security, take a deep breath and celebrate the fact that they're going to allow you to use that ticket you paid for. But don't get excited. You need to remain calm for the boarding process. I'm guessing, based on your spending patterns, that you're in the cheap seats, which means right at the back of the plane—let's say seat 37B. Once the kids and fake limpers get on the plane, they usually board from the back.

They'll announce, "Anybody sitting in Row 30 or higher, please step forward." Surprisingly, everyone with a ticket will then step forward—regardless of what row they're sitting in. That's because they're afraid that they're going to get this close and yet not be able to get on—like maybe the airline oversold the flight or somebody made a clerical mistake or maybe they just don't like the look of you. It's not really that they don't expect the clerk to let them on, it's just their way of letting everybody know that they're here and that they're not going away until they get on that airplane. So you'll need to push by all of those wannabes and get yourself on that plane.

- As soon as you get on the plane, before you go to your seat, use the restroom. Even if you don't have to go, it's always good to bank one. Again, based on your spending history, you're probably in a middle seat between a sleeping senior and really fat guy. You're locked in for the long haul.

- After everybody gets on the plane, and even though you're expecting the flight to take an hour and a half, the captain will come on the P.A. and announce that today's flying time will be thirty-seven minutes. You're delighted because that means the flight is only half as long as you thought. Thirty minutes later, when you're still taxiing, you'll realize it was a cruel joke. The thirty-seven minutes was kind of like the online computer repair suggestions you get—statistically correct but totally useless.

- The flight will go fine. In fact, it may even go better than expected. That's always a bad thing. The captain will come on again and say we've made great time and will be arriving eleven minutes early. Later, when you notice the plane has stopped and you're nowhere near the terminal, the captain will try to hide his glee as he announces that the gate isn't ready because we're so early. To me, it seems odd how the arrival of the plane that the control tower has been guiding for the last ninety minutes can somehow be a surprise.

The bottom line: you have no reasonable alternatives. As unpleasant as air travel might be, it's the quickest, most cost-effective way to get anywhere. So just suck it up, pack light—and wash your feet.

HOW TO SPOT YOUR ENEMIES

There's an expression that says, "Keep your friends close, but keep your enemies closer." I think it was started by a deodorant company. But the point of it is, you always want to know who your enemies are so that you can watch what they're doing. Often in life, it's much easier to spot your friends than your enemies. That's because they are more obvious and there are usually fewer of them. So here's a quick checklist of warning signs that a certain person is not your friend:

- They own the house you live in.
- They stop smiling when they see you.
- They call the police when they see you.
- When they talk to you they're always holding a tire iron.
- They often refer to a power tool you borrowed.
- You just backed into their car.
- You owe them money.
- You're the reason their lawn smells bad.
- They ask you to do things.
- They tell you to do things.

- They complain to your wife about the things you didn't do.
- They complain to your wife about the things you did do.

HOW TO FIX A LEAKY FAUCET

This is not a euphemism. We're talking about an actual leaky faucet—like, say, the one in your kitchen sink that's released more drips than the National Accounting School. Well, the time has come for you to fix it. Ninety per cent of tap leaks come from the rubber washers inside that have gotten brittle or cracked. It could be from the impurities in your water or it could just be old age. When was the last time you replaced the washers? If you can't remember, that could also just be old age. In any case, replacing them is a good place to start when trying to repair a leaky faucet. Here's what to do.

1) Put on your bathing suit. Things are going to get wet. You may be tempted to put on your *birthday* suit, but if the house floods and you have to run out onto the front lawn, that can be embarrassing. Especially if the water's cold.

2) Close the shut-off valves under the sink before taking the faucet apart. If you installed the shut-off valves, it might be a good idea to also shut off the main water

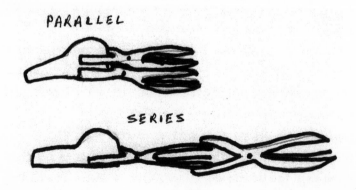

PARALLEL

SERIES

valve in the basement. If you helped your neighbours install their valves, call the town and have them shut off the whole street.

3) Remove the faucet handles. This can be tricky, because over the years they can become glued on with bits of pasta and hardened cheese. Try tapping them with a rubber hammer so you don't scratch the chrome. If you don't have a rubber hammer, use a croquet mallet. If that doesn't work, slit open a tennis ball or a dog toy and slide it over the handle. Then apply Vise-Grips and twist it off. If necessary, you can use two sets of Vise-Grips, in parallel or in series (see diagram).

4) Remove the valve stem with an open-ended or adjustable wrench. If you're standing in the sink with one foot up against the wall for added leverage and it still doesn't loosen, it's probably a left-hand thread. Try going the other way.

5) Once the valve stem is removed, undo the machine screw at the bottom so that you can get at the washer. It may seem like petrified wood, but at one time it was rubber. If the screwdriver is too wide to pry it out, you can break it into pieces using one of those fancy metal picks that came with your walnut bowl. Just make sure you get all the little bits out. It's okay to blow on it, but make sure your eyes are closed.

6) Insert the new rubber washers into the valve stems and snug up the machine screw. Before reinstalling the stems, clean up the valve seat. If you're made of money, there's a special tool for that job, but I would suggest you just use your thumbnail. Then tighten the valve stems and reattach the handles.

7) Put the taps into the off position and turn the water back on using all the levels of water-flow management that were engaged at the start of the job. Most manuals tell

you to then check the job for leaks, but I advise against this. It will only lead to disappointment and humiliation. Instead, just assume that the operation was successful. If it wasn't, you'll find out soon enough.

THE COMPUTER IS YOUR FRIEND

I know you probably find computers frustrating because they behave in ways you don't understand, aren't always reliable and let you down when you need them most. Here's a way to feel a lot better about all of that. Instead of thinking of the computer as a robot, or even as a tool, think of it as your friend.

Remember when you first met a friend? How fascinating you found him? He was quick and easy to get along with and he would do pretty much whatever you wanted. Then, as time went by, he started to slow down, he'd take a long time to warm up and would sometimes be completely unresponsive. But if you're going to point the finger of blame, start with yourself. Look at all the crazy things you've asked your computer to do:

- just sit there taking dictation while you typed in the most inarticulate correspondence in the history of the English language;
- download and install three hundred megabytes of anti-virus software while you simultaneously surfed all the XXX websites;
- print off a thirty-page document with 3D graphics while you tried to get some photo software to magically focus a picture you took;
- scan twenty-five thousand files looking for a document you lost, and all you could remember about it was that it had the word BUT in the text;

- survive a can of Mountain Dew spilled into the keyboard;
- spend a night in Alaska in the trunk of the car;
- be used to pry open the screen door;
- have an incident involving gravity and a concrete floor;
- operate a webcam with bad lighting so that relatives in Europe could see how ugly you are.

I think once you see how you've abused this friend over the years, you'll realize it has been reasonably loyal and is doing the best that can be expected under the circumstances. Hopefully people are saying the same thing about you.

PAUSE FOR THOUGHTS: SOME WORDS OF WISDOM

To cure a spoiled child, give him a skateboard or a gallon of prune juice. Either one will teach him about consequences.

The beauty of being unemployed is that you never have to suffer the humiliation of a pay cut.

How to save between 10 and 15 per cent annually on your food and beverage costs: don't tip.

The Idiot Rule: If you identify ten unrelated persons as idiots within any one-month period, chances are you have overestimated the number of idiots by nine, and the guilty party is not one of the ten.

If I had a dollar for every stupid thing I've done, that would have encouraged me to do a lot more stupid things.

Taking Viagra is a bad business decision. You're creating a supply for which there is no demand.

God plays golf. Bald spots are just Him not replacing his divots.

Being married for over forty years makes me believe that world peace is still possible.

I meant to procrastinate today, but I never got around to it.

CHOOSING THE CORRECT FASTENER

Eighty per cent of every project involves putting things together. (The rest is 10 per cent building the pieces and 10 per cent applying the bandages.) So for those of you who have not embraced duct tape as the Handyman's Secret Weapon, you have a lot of thinking to do. Deciding exactly how you're going to attach the pieces to each other is often the most important aspect of the entire project.

There are a wide variety of fasteners available, each of which is designed for a specific application.

> Standard nails. Nails are the quickest, cheapest and easiest way to attach most things to other things, but they do have several inadequacies. They are most effective going into wood, less so going into concrete, and if you're trying to drive a nail into a steel I-beam, you obviously have a severe mental problem. Even with wood, nails are most effective in preventing lateral movement, like when a stud is attached to a header. They have virtually no tensile holding ability, as you discover when you put a nail into the ceiling and hang a chandelier from it. Choosing the length and thickness of a nail is also important. Trying to hammer a ¼-inch diameter nail into a $^5/_{16}$-inch piece of trim is probably not going to go well. The length is also a factor, as the nail needs to go far

enough into the wall that it will hold up your painting, but not far enough into the wall that it removes your neighbour's painting.

Specialty nails. Drywall nails, spiral nails, concrete nails, etc.—this is all just mutton dressed as lamb. These nails have small barbs on the shaft, or spiral threads to help them hold, but they're still easy to pull out. Concrete nails are too hard to bend, which often makes them too hard to hit.

Screws. Definitely a step up from nails, screws come in a wide range of types and materials and have a lot more tensile strength than any nail. They're slower to install, but much safer. Nobody ever hit their thumb with a screwdriver.

Bolts. We're getting serious now. All of the good points of nails and screws, with much more tensile strength. If you put an eyebolt through the kitchen ceiling with a washer the size of a dinner plate and a locking nut on top, you can hang a side of buffalo meat on it. The drawback of bolts is that you must have access to both sides of the surface. It's like selling magazine subscriptions by phone—you need to have a nut on the other end.

So that's more or less the range of available fasteners, and you may still be wondering which of them is best for your job and what size should you get and all the rest of it. Well, it's really just basic physics. What forces are in play and what direction are they pulling?

If you're mounting a picture on the wall, you have tangential gravitational pull equal to the picture's weight. Even a small nail will do the job. If you're hanging a full suit of armour, the three-dimensional aspect of it will create a horizontal tensile pull, making a nail unfeasible, so you'll have to go with the heftiest screw you can find. (Let's pause for a second and make up our own punch lines.) If you're wealthy enough to own a double-wide, you have access to both sides of the wall and can therefore use a bolt.

The general rule with fasteners is that if they're stronger than the wall or ceiling they're attached to, when there's an overload (like Uncle Bob doing his Tarzan impersonation from your chandelier), you want the fastener to let go, rather than the structure to collapse. So before attaching anything to anything, assess the structural integrity of the anchoring wall, and use a fastener that's just slightly weaker than that. That's the way to get maximum strength from your fastener without putting your security deposit at risk.

THE DANGERS OF THE "TO DO" LIST

Every handyman encounters a "to do" list many times in his life. If he's married, it's not even in his own handwriting. But most handymen fail to realize that there's an art to making a "to do" list that strikes just the right balance between dreams and reality. Here are a few guidelines to keep in mind whenever you or a loved one is making a "to do" list.

1) Number the items, and limit the number. A "to do" list with more than six items is just a trial separation waiting to happen. Large print on a small piece of paper will automatically shorten the list, while making it easier to read and small enough to carry in your pocket.

2) The items on the list should each be roughly within the limits of the knowledge base, skill level and healing capacity of the person who's expected to do them. An item like "repair wave generator in microwave oven" is just asking for trouble.

3) Prorate the number of words to the difficulty of the task. Instead of a list that says:
    - Change light bulb on porch
    - Install new furnace

It needs to say:

- Change light bulb on porch
- Shut off gas to old furnace
- Disconnect ductwork and electrical power
- Disassemble old furnace
- Remove old furnace parts and take to dump or give to Uncle Bob
- Assemble new furnace
- Connect ductwork and electrical power
- Turn on gas
- Call fire department

4) Whoever has to do the work gets to assign time estimates for each task. A light bulb change would get five minutes (ten if there's a fixture), but a stove repair would get six hours and building a deck would get four months.

5) Prioritize the jobs. After the handyman has done the time estimates, he needs to return the list to the author so that she can put the jobs in the order she wants them done. If she opts for starting several jobs at once, it needs to be understood that the time estimates for all of the selected jobs will become the same as the longest job—i.e., it will now take you four months to change the light bulb.

6) Set boundaries. A weekend has sixteen available hours in which to do stuff. But it's also your weekend, so you shouldn't feel you have to give them all up. Allow time for rest and meals and football games. I suggest that four hours of handyman work on any given weekend will get enough done to keep the family happy and still prevent you from dreading weekends. This negotiation can be tough if you haven't done anything constructive for the last 168 weekends, which puts you 672 hours in arrears on your handyman commitment. You may need a lawyer.

SAFETY RULES FOR THE HANDYMAN

Every specialty has its own set of rules and regulations, and being a handyman is no exception. Here is a small sampling of safety rules that can help you retire with the same number of fingers you started with.

- When you operate a buzz saw, keep one hand behind your back.
- When you're using a hammer from the kneeling position, make sure your buddy isn't standing behind you.
- Before you switch on a powerful electromagnet, remove your steel-toed work boots. Also check that your car keys haven't fallen into your underwear.
- If you're wearing a tie while operating a lathe, make sure it's a clip-on.
- If you see lightning, move away from the tall guy.
- Do not spray water on a chemical fire, no matter how nervous you get.
- Wearing seatbelts is good, but it's even safer if your vehicle has doors.
- Don't eat spicy food if you share a small office.
- A gas-powered auger works by you holding the handle steady while the bit spins into the ground. As soon as the bit jams on a rock, that process will be reversed.
- Never carry any kind of pinching tool in your pants pocket.
- Most metal-fabricating tools can do things to your finger that you wouldn't have thought possible.
- Solder and facial hair is not a good combination.
- Never get caught between electricity and where it wants to go.
- Watching a punch press too closely resulted in the world's most painful nose-piercing.

- Never let down your guard, particularly the one on the table saw.
- It is easier to clear metal filings off your safety glasses with a soft brush than it is to pull them out of your eye with a pair of tweezers.
- Before you try arc welding, take off your wedding ring.
- Whenever two guys are working together, there are far fewer accidents if the big guy holds the spike while the little guy swings the hammer.
- Keep your workshop clean so the cuts won't get infected.

THE MIRACLE OF MECHANICAL ADVANTAGE

There is a branch of science that can be very helpful to the handyman. I'm talking about physics. Not psychics, not psychos, but *physics*: the science of how bodies move and interact. The study of physics has been around for several hundred years now, so even people from the Midwest are ready to try it. And of all the services physics has to offer, there's none more helpful than a little thing called mechanical advantage.

Mechanical advantage is the fundamental building block of Sir Isaac Newton's six simple machines. If you study them, you'll come up with all kinds of creative ways to do ridiculous things with great ease. Let me give you an example. Let's say you need to lift a 440-cubic-inch Dodge hemi V8 out of a '72 Challenger so that you can rebuild it. If you have an A-frame and a motorized block and tackle, you have no problem. But if you have those things, you sound like a person who knows what they're doing, so you're probably not reading this book. I want to talk to the guy who has a handful of clothesline pulleys and a 9-volt cordless drill. He's the one who needs the help.

Okay. First of all, you need to understand a couple of basic principles. Mechanical advantage works by converting speed into power, which allows you to do something difficult while accepting that it will be done more slowly. For example, if the cordless drill had enough torque to lift the engine, you could just wrap a chain around a bit, secure the drill to the ceiling, turn it on and pop that engine right out of there. But that's impossible because the drill is only capable of generating one-quarter of a foot-pound of torque at full rpm, while the engine weighs more than two hundred pounds. This is where the clothesline pulleys come in. Hook one up as shown here:

Because the ratio of the diameter of the bit to the diameter of the pulley is about ten to one, the pulley goes around once for every ten times the drill goes around. The good news is the torque is increased by the same ratio—ten times. So now we're getting 2.5 foot-pounds of torque. Now add another step:

The ratio is compounded, so the drill has to go around a hundred times for the second pulley to go around once. But the torque at the axle of the second pulley is now up to 25 foot-pounds. Just one more step to go:

The drill has to go around a thousand times for the last pulley to go around once, but we're now generating 250 foot-pounds of torque, which is enough to lift the engine. Secure the drill and pulleys to the garage ceiling with lag bolts, or duct tape in an overlapping pattern. Attach the chain to the axle of the last pulley and wrap it around the engine. At full speed, the drill will be turning at 360 rpm, which means the last axle will be turning at 0.36 rpm. If the circumference of the axle is three-quarters of an inch, the engine will be rising at the rate of 0.27 inches per minute. You'll need to raise the engine high enough to clear the radiator, which is

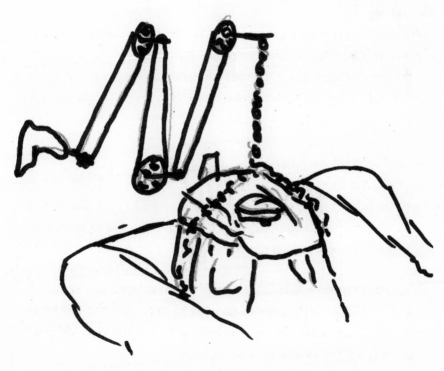

a distance of about 32 inches, which will take you about two hours of full drill power. That's where the trade-off of speed for power comes in. A couple of final suggestions: have a few fully charged drill batteries on hand, and practise changing them really, really fast. Also, be sure to undo the motor mounts.

QUICK TIP #9: SEALING A DRAFTY WINDOW

Stuff the cracks around a drafty window with cheese. Mice will eat it and then get stuck from the weight gain. That's what you want, because mice have an R-value of 34, whereas cheese is only R-15. Repeat as necessary.

PASSING THE TORCH

There is nothing more satisfying in the life of a handyman than to see the day when he can pass the torch to his son or daughter. Someone to continue the tradition of taking on projects for which they have no training. It brings a tear to your eye to watch your own child display the attitude that any fix-it challenge can be handled with a little common sense, a dash of ingenuity and a large roll of duct tape. The best way to have such an experience is to identify the handyman potential in your kids, then nurture it. If you have more than one child, you will probably find that only one has the handyman gene. The other child will be more like your wife and is pretty much guaranteed a successful life, but the one like you is going to need all the help they can get. Your job is to spot the tendencies early. Here are some things to watch for that will identify a child as the next family handyman.

- They take all their toys apart before they play with them.
- They turn the clock around to face the wall because they don't care what time it is, they'd rather see how it works.
- They get a model wooden boat and then smash it into pieces to build a raft.
- At their first family picnic, they use a 48-inch pipe wrench to open a jar of pickles.
- They ask for two toboggans for Christmas so they can flip one over and use it as a ski jump.
- After one too many flat tires on their bike, they remove the inner tube and fill the tire with silicon caulk.
- To get more power out of their Super Soaker, they pump it up with an industrial air compressor.
- They have the patience to cook a hot dog with a magnifying glass.
- They have an extremely high pain threshold.
- They borrow your tools and don't return them.
- They spend their allowance at the auto wrecker's.
- If a crescent wrench is a little too big, they will wedge a flat screwdriver into the gap and make it work.
- They set off fireworks on Arbor Day.
- They prefer function over form. As long as it works, who cares what it looks like? Whenever they build, repair or renovate, they do almost all of it out of existing garage inventory.

- When their names come up in a conversation, people shake their heads.
- They join Possum Lodge.

CRISIS MANAGEMENT

Accidents and other unexpected events occur in the lives of everyone, and the trick to managing them properly is to be able to quickly evaluate the severity of the situation and select the response that effectively solves the problem with a minimum of collateral damage. To help you learn how to pick the appropriate responses, I've created five stages of crises, with examples for each. You will never completely eliminate embarrassment or ridicule from your life, but with a little training, you can minimize their frequency and severity.

STAGE ONE CRISIS: Property Loss or Damage, No Personal Injury and No Witnesses

Nobody saw you do what you did. You know it was stupid. You know there'll be problems later. But right now it's your little secret. So what should you do? Nothing. Absolutely nothing. Duck and cover. Time is your friend. The longer you can get away with whatever you did, the more lenient the judgment against you will be.

Say, for example, your wife left her diamond bracelet on top of the toilet, and while you were standing there with one hand free, you picked it up to look at it. Then, while you were flushing with that same hand, the bracelet dropped into the whirlpool rapids and was whisked away forever on a wave of urine. Do you tell your wife what happened? No. You wait. You wait until she mentions it. And it will be a while. Because when she can't find it, she won't want to tell you. So she'll look everywhere, all over the house, in the car, in the yard—everywhere. Then she'll call all of

146

her friends to see if she left it at their homes. Finally, as a last resort, she'll ask you if you've seen her bracelet, and you answer honestly, "No, I haven't seen it in a long time." There'll be a few more days of searching, and then finally she will tell you that she's lost her diamond bracelet. You will then take her in your arms and tell her not to be upset and that you will gladly buy her another one. If you get guilt pangs, you can promise yourself that you will tell her the truth on your death bed. In fact, whenever you tell her, it *will* be your death bed.

STAGE TWO CRISIS: Personal Injury, No Property Loss or Damage and No Witnesses

You've hurt yourself doing something that was not only stupid, it was something your friends and family warned you not to do. And now you're injured, but the most painful aspect of the injury is admitting you were wrong. Here, again, the lack of witnesses is a key component.

Let's say you decided you could take down the old garden shed on your own and you hit yourself in the knee with a sledgehammer. Just lie quietly until you get the pain under control and then practise walking normally. Go into the house and ask your wife if she has any jobs she'd like you to do. Out of the list, pick the one that requires the most physical exertion—like, say, moving the piano. Start trying to move it on your own, and then yell out in pain. Omigosh, you've just thrown your knee out! And you did it trying to please your wife. You're going to be offered a lot of sympathy, so be a man—take it.

STAGE THREE CRISIS: Property Loss or Damage or Personal Injury with Witnesses

This is the day you need to prepare for way ahead of time. Just going willy-nilly into an adventure with an open invitation to all of your friends—or worse still, people you don't even know—is asking for a level of scrutiny that will only work against you.

So it's very important that you put a lot of preparatory work into selecting the people that are okay to be there when you do something foolish. You will have had plenty of opportunities to meet people like that. Maybe they were your buddies at school, or maybe you met them at work. The key component is that they see things the same way you do and would be likely to try the same stunt themselves if you hadn't volunteered. In fact, the best way to befriend them is to be there when they tried some ridiculous project that failed—then they owe you one. Friendship and loyalty are lofty goals, but somebody who owes you one is someone you can count on. These are the only people you want in attendance when you try barefoot waterskiing for the first time, even though your workout regimen has been limited to twisting caps off beer bottles —which, coincidentally, was done just prior to the waterskiing episode. When the property damage and personal injury issues come forward, you need to be surrounded by people who will corroborate you story. Witnesses that don't know you—or worse, don't owe you—will be a problem.

STAGE FOUR CRISIS: Unlimited Property Damage

It's one thing to suffer a forehead abrasion from the barbecue lid as it rockets skyward because you started the grill without opening it, but when that same lid comes crashing back down to the same place—which gravity without wind will often make possible— shattering the propane fittings and sending a fireball into the wooden fence that is now burning in both directions as it heads towards your neighbours on either side, the option of not saying anything has gone out the window. The best thing to do is to tell a friend—or, failing that, a neighbour, or, failing *that*, your wife—to call the fire department and tell them to drop by with hoses ASAP. Then go lie down in the middle of the backyard, pretend the lid knocked you out and hope for the best. It's probably not going to go well.

STAGE FIVE CRISIS: Unlimited Personal Injury

I'm guessing that if your actions injured other people, it would really bother you, unless you're a stockbroker. As in Stage Four, you really need to step back and ask yourself, "If this goes bad, how bad can it get?" When you destroy your own property or injure yourself, that was obviously a risk you were willing to take. When you destroy other people's property or injure innocent bystanders, that's not a good day. You know yourself that you would never choose to be victimized by anyone else's stupidity. In fact, you don't need to be because your own stupidity is more than adequate. What you need is a personal disclaimer—a formal announcement that anyone within a certain radius of your personality could be injured. If they choose to stay out of morbid curiosity or a potential TV deal with Fox, then they have to accept responsibility for their own safety. If you don't give them fair warning, you'll be reading this book in prison.

SHADES OF GREEN

These days everybody's going green. But are you green enough? Try the following quiz to see how you measure up—whether you're part of the solution or part of the problem that will lead to the end of the human race.

1) How do you get up in the morning?
   Worst Response: The clock radio blasts out heavy metal rock music, you turn the shower to full hot while you run around the house turning all the lights on.
   Better Response: The wind-up alarm clock rings in your ear, you get up using a flashlight and wash your face in cold water.
   Best Response: You wait for the sun to both wake you

and light the house, and then you give yourself a light dusting with your pajama bottoms.

2) How do you prepare breakfast?
Worst Response: Bacon and eggs in an electric frypan, coffee from your espresso maker and two pieces of over-cooked toast from your twelve-slice toaster.
Better Response: Instant coffee from an electric kettle, with a bagel warmed up by wedging it in the handle.
Best Response: A handful of granola washed down by drinking well water directly from the hand pump.

3) How do you get to work?
Worst Response: Driving a twenty-five-year-old full-size van with a big-block V8 that burns oil and a cargo area full of cement bags and car parts.
Better Response: Public transit, preferably an electric streetcar or trolley bus.
Best Response: Phone in sick.

4) How do you maintain your lawn and garden?
Worst Response: Mowing with a 12-horsepower garden tractor, controlling the dandelions with Roundup and killing voles with bags of DDT.
Better Response: A push mower, watering the lawn and fertilizing the garden.
Best Response: Doing nothing. Declaring the yard a pro-tected, chemical- and maintenance-free environmental area.

5) How do you spend your evenings?
Worst Response: Drinking beer on the patio around a tire fire.
Better Response: Watching TV with only one light on.

Best Response: Dropping in on your neighbour's at dinnertime and going to bed at sunset.

6) What does a good environmentalist do?
Worst Response: Wait for the government to fix everything.
Better Response: Reduce, reuse, renew.
Best Response: Instead of putting out garbage, make a massive compost heap in the yard and then use the flies to catch fish.

THE MILLION-DOLLAR HANDYMAN

When you look at the richest people in the world, you will very rarely find a handyman among them. That's because historically a handyman's way is not to amass wealth, but rather to make the most of what he has. A handyman is a person who enjoys a very comfortable lifestyle without ever generating anything above an average annual income.

Let's take a minute now to appreciate some of the ways the handyman in your home adds value to your life.

By his ability to fix things for the cost of the parts. Add up all the repair bills you didn't have to pay over a thirty-year period. It will be a big number. All the car repairs and appliance repairs and roof repairs and plumbing leaks and electrical malfunctions and lawn-mower service, etc., etc. And what did it cost you? Just a bunch of weekends, a few replacement parts and a hundred or so rolls of duct tape. A small price to pay. Estimated lifetime saving: $50,000.

By his ability to make smarter purchases. A handyman is never afraid to buy something used, because he's pretty good at evaluating its current condition and is confident he can fix it when it breaks. They say a new car loses 20 per cent of its value once you drive it off the lot, but the non-handyman is forced to pay that price because he needs the warranty to make up for his incompetence. Three years later, when the warranty is done, he'll sell the car for peanuts, and the person who will give him those peanuts will be a handyman. Estimated lifetime saving: $100,000.

By his ability to fix up a home that's a "fixer-upper." There are probably a few neighbourhoods in your town that you can't afford to buy a house in. You just don't have enough household income to pay the mortgage on a $500,000 home. But if any of those subdivisions has a fixer-upper, and you have a handyman, you're movin' on up. Just give him a $100,000 mortgage and twenty years and he'll turn that place into a gem. That guy with the greasy hands and the tool belt is your ticket to the good life. Estimated lifetime saving: $400,000.

By his ability to make friends with wealthy people. Generally speaking, rich people are useless with their hands. So once you've moved into the fixer-upper in their neighbourhood, you can start doing little freebie repair jobs for them and they will use you and respect you—but mainly use you. It's not because of the money you save them, it's the time. When their cappuccino maker blows a breaker, they're not going to see the serviceman for a week or so. You can be there in ten minutes and hit the reset and tell them not to turn on the iron and the toaster oven while they're making coffee, and they'll look at you like you're Donald Trump. Suddenly, you're fixing the swimming pool pump and the beer cooler and the sauna, and then you get to invite a few friends over to try them out. You get all the perks of high-end living without any of the costs. Estimated lifetime saving: $100,000.

By his ability to be indispensable. If you take a look at an average block in an urban community, you will find that most of the residents are professional people (lawyers, accountants, medical professionals), some are unionized skilled labourers (welders, plumbers, electricians), fewer still are unskilled labourers (ditch diggers, crossing guards, politicians) and the smallest number of all are handymen—people who have enough basic knowledge of everything to be able to fix anything. When people find out you're a handyman, you immediately go to the "A" list. They will like you even if they don't like you. That's because, for the first time in your life, the law of supply and demand is on your side. Use it wisely. Help everybody, including yourself. Don't be afraid to take a gift from them, or even money. They will call you again, and whatever you turn down now will not be offered later. Estimated value of being indispensable: $100,000.

By his ability to feel no fear. Any handyman who is still alive after ten years of fixing things has learned a lot, and if he still has the use of all of his fingers, he can apply that knowledge to any future repairs. But the main advantage he has is that he is relatively unafraid to tackle any of life's problems, either mechanical or emotional. He is the master of his domain. And that confidence permeates his family and friends and helps them have the courage to take on challenges that might otherwise overwhelm them. So here's to you, Mr. Handyman, making this a better world for all of us as you take it all on with nothing more than a cocky smile, a roll of duct tape and a hospitalization card. Estimated value of being fearless: $250,000.

HOW TO CATCH MICE

Almost every home, at one time or another, is going to have at least one mouse in it. Often unwanted. The level of infestation can vary based on many factors such as the integrity of the foundation, the integrity of the pest-control initiatives and, most importantly, the integrity of the owner. Now, maybe you feel that mice have every right to be in your home, or that one of them is the reincarnated version of your Uncle Bob, so you don't want to do anything about the problem. That's fine with me, but you should know that mice procreate at a tremendous rate, as do most things that don't have cable television. You will find in time that mice will be in all the floors and walls, will eat all your groceries and will start moving furniture around. And I don't care how cute you think mice are; when one runs across your face in the middle of the night, you'll be wanting to take the mickey out of Walt Disney. So here are a few simple steps that you can take to at least control the rodent population in your home.

Extermination. From having a cat, to the simple mousetrap, to bags of poison, the goal is the same: to send as many furry residents as possible to mouse heaven. The trouble with cats is they tend to have their own agenda. The problem with the mousetrap is that what you catch most often is your own finger. Or you find you're dealing with a very smart mouse who is capable of licking the bait off the trigger without setting off the trap. The other downside is that when you catch a mouse, you have to deal with it. I've heard of squeamish people who just throw the whole trap away with the mouse still in it. This is very expensive, and the steel spring wrapped around its neck impedes the mouse's biodegradability. Sometimes the trap just catches one foot, so the mouse starts dragging it around the kitchen floor like Jacob Marley. That doesn't make for a very nice Christmas.

Bags of poison are more effective and less work because the mouse gets so thirsty he leaves the house in search of water to drink, which in this case is literally last call. But poison is expensive, and dangerous if you have a dog, especially a small, mousy dog. Extermination is final in that it kills the mouse in question, but it does not kill all the mice that have access to your home. That's more like genocide—which, historically, has not been beneficial to either side.

Catch and release. I'm talking about those sticky sheets of goo or those fancy maze traps where the mouse falls into a tiny chamber where he stays until you let him out. The sticky pads are messy, and it's hard to get the mouse off once he's stuck on there. And if you accidentally sit on one as you come out of the shower, you will be reminded that almost all body parts have hair on them. The other issue is the release. You need to take the mouse far enough away that he won't just slip between your legs and run back into the house. You will find yourself firing up your van and doing a weekly mouse run to the far end of town. And when you explain what you're doing to the cop who just pulled you over, there's not a chance in the world that he'll think you're sober.

Infestation prevention. Many people think they can prevent mouse problems simply by blocking all the cracks and holes in the foundation of their home. It was true when the home was originally built—say, in the early '50s—but by now the mice have proliferated to the point that they no longer need immigrants to sustain their society. Their short gestation period and lack of birth control allow them to flourish without any access to the world outside your home. Also, the holes mice get in through are similar to the ones they get out through, so plugging them does as much to keep mice in as it does to keep them out.

Creating options. Mice are not stupid, particularly when compared to many of my friends. A mouse will always choose the path that brings the greatest success with the least effort. Let's say you have a mouse in the yard between your house and your neighbour's. There's a 50/50 chance that he'll come into your home. But you can improve those odds dramatically if you give your neighbour a 100-pound wheel of cheese and recommend he keep it in his basement. The same approach works for mice already in your house. Don't put down bags of poison in the rec room; use bags of marshmallows. As long as you make it unnecessary for mice to come to the kitchen, they'll never be there. They don't enjoy your cooking any more than you do.

Make a stand. Instead of focusing on the rooms that have mice in them, identify the ones that don't. They'll be the ones without chew marks on the furniture legs, or scampering noises in the walls, or HAVE A NICE DAY written on the floor in mouse droppings. Next, move into one of those rooms and make it your base camp. Then slowly over time you will fan out from that room, military style, using every weapon available at your disposal, as described above. You'll feel the momentum build as you take back the bathroom, then the guest room, the living room, the dining room and, ultimately, the kitchen. You may never eradicate the mice, but you will eventually build an understanding that you have your space and they have theirs. And the world will be a better place.

THE DEMANDS OF BOAT OWNERSHIP

Every day, innocent people buy boats with absolutely no idea of what they're getting into. Other than getting married or having kids, there is not a bigger monkey wrench you can throw into your life than a boat. Not a car. Not a house. Not a swimming pool. Not even a video game. Boats are pretty demanding.

The reason is simple: boats live in a hostile environment. Oh sure, you think they float on the water, and what could possibly be the problem? Well, my friend, they only float as long as they displace their own weight. The moment their displacement shrinks (like a leak below the waterline) or their weight increases (a minute after the leak below the waterline), they don't float anymore. All boats are living on borrowed time. You may think your house or your car needs more maintenance than a boat. You are so wrong it's embarrassing. You can let your house rot for a year or two. You can let your car rust in the backyard. They'll still be there when you get around to them. Not so with a boat. A boat is like a woman you love: if you want to keep her, you can't be thinking she'll be there when you get around to her. She's there now. That's all you get.

So before you make a commitment to a boat, you need two things: an understanding wife and an understanding boss. (If these two are the same person, you've lucked out—but only in this area.) If your wife is not interested in a boat, don't buy it. If you've already bought it, sell it—and be prepared to take a bath on the price. The most expensive boat experience is generally cheaper than the cheapest divorce experience. But if your wife is okay with it, you're halfway there.

Now you need your boss to buy into the idea that you having a boat makes you a better employee. And it does, considering you now have to generate enough income to support your problem. I'm not guessing here. I've had this disease for the last fifty years, and I have an understanding wife and am sort of self-employed, but even so, when you add up the dock fees and the winter storage and the insurance and the MAINTENANCE—let me say that again, the MAINTENANCE—the numbers make no sense. Heroin addicts probably have better cash flow than boat owners.

And yet here we are. A band of lunatics who think there's something special about being on the water. I have nothing more to say because, and it hurts me to say this, I'm writing this on my boat and there is no place I would rather be. It's too late for me. Save yourself if you can.

HANDYMAN FINGERPRINTS

You can learn a lot about the attitudes and personality of a handyman just by looking at his repair job. That's because repair work is a creative endeavour, a combination of art and engineering. And whenever a person gets creative, they reveal their innermost feelings. Let me give you an example:

Here's a car side mirror whose housing got broken due to a confrontation with the door frame while someone was backing out of the garage. The traditional repair would be to use a high-powered automotive glue like this:

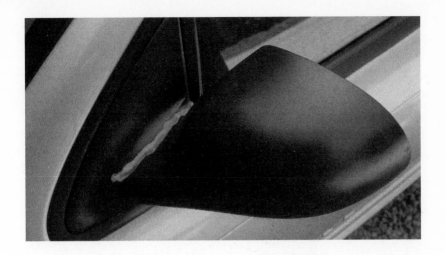

That's the sign of a conventional, non-creative thinker. The kind of person who would seek out expert advice and then follow it. This is not the kind of approach that leads to an interesting life. On the practical side, all glues dry out in the sun, and winter temperatures make them brittle, but the main drawback is that the deterioration of the glue is not always obvious, so one good pothole and there goes your mirror. The better solution, of course, is duct tape, but even then the technique says a lot about the technician:

This guy is an optimist.

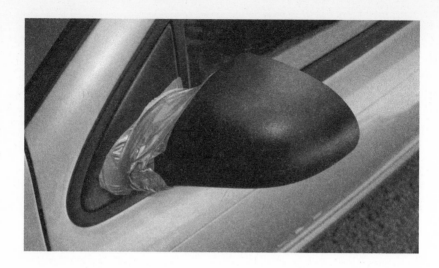

This is a sensible, logical guy who obviously has other things to do today.

This is a person who is good at analyzing stress points and vectors but gets very cautious when choosing counteractive measures to overcome those problems. They suffer from a lack of self-confidence, which they project onto their repair work.

This is a subtle addition to the cautious approach and could even be a sub-category of it. The key separating factor is the lack of intelligence and foresight that would allow this handyman to extend the repair job beyond the edges of the car door, making it inoperable. This person does not understand cause and effect and should not be given power tools.

This person has a severe inferiority complex and is using the repair job as an opportunity to show off. And if sending the message "Hey, I'm an idiot," qualifies as showing off, they have succeeded.

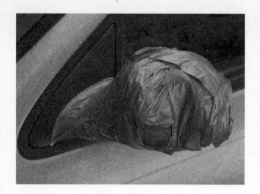

This person is a small thinker. They were so focused on the current problem of securing a cracked housing that they lost sight of the big picture: having a functional side mirror. This approach of technically solving the immediate problem but having an overall long-term negative effect usually indicates that the person responsible is in the medical profession.

DECIDING WHO SHOULD PAY THE BILLS

This is one of the icebergs. It's way bigger than it looks. Almost everything else in life is way *smaller* than it looks. Most couples don't realize it, but deciding who should pay the bills is often the most complex aspect of their relationship. I've heard people say the other person is better at math, but keeping the books in order does not have much to do with math. If something costs a dime and you've only got a nickel in your pocket, no mathematician in the world can close that deal.

It's not about math, it's about maturity—the maturity to quantify the amount of money coming in while anticipating the amount of money going out, to make sure the first number is bigger than the second, and to do all that without being snarky. That takes a grown-up. The unfortunate corollary of this arrangement is that the other person becomes the child. In any relationship, the person who controls the money is in charge. The person who doesn't, isn't.

Let's say, for example, your wife has been managing the books ever since that summer you lost your job and then used your income tax refund for the deposit on a boat. So now you hand over every paycheque to your wife and, other than the pocket money which she calls your "disposable income" but is actually your allowance, she decides where and when the money goes. And, of course, once you have no control over something, you immediately lose all interest in it. Soon you lose all connection between the money you are contributing and the lifestyle you are enjoying. You don't think about the mortgage and taxes that are being paid. You don't think about the phone and utility bills that are being taken care of on time. You're not aware that your credit card debt is under control. All you know is you hand over your paycheque every week and you're not being allowed to buy a motorcycle.

Another, more subtle, side effect is the inequity of information access. Marriage is about sharing equally. Under these circumstances, your wife knows exactly how much you make and how much you spend, which is fine. However, you don't have a clue about her finances, which is okay when addressing joint expenditures like rent and services, but can be problematic when you get to discretionary spending. Maybe the money she spends on having her hair and nails done every week should be used to buy power tools. (I'm saying this as an example of how problems start. I'm not suggesting that you tell your wife to nix the manicure so you can buy a nail gun.)

What all of this boils down to is something that applies to most aspects of a relationship: the need to communicate. There need to be regular meetings between you and your chief financial officer (wife) where you can discuss the current fiscal status and set policy. The decision to have her handle the money is logical and will help you avoid prison time. But she needs to respect your entitlement to review the plan and make suggestions. As long as you know what's going on, you will avoid feelings of resentment and begin to appreciate what your wife is doing for both of you.

The flow of information is the key. Knowledge is power. At the next meeting, ask her when you'll be able to buy a motorcycle and she'll say never and you won't even flinch because in your heart you know that's the best answer for her, for you and for all of the members of your community.

HOW TO TELL IF YOU'RE BORING

There are all kinds of ways to become more interesting. They teach courses on it—how to ask engaging questions, how to be socially adept, all that stuff. But the reason most people don't bother is that they're not motivated to improve socially. And the reason for that is they don't realize how boring they are. The first step in solving any problem is acknowledging there actually *is* a problem. So here are the signs you should watch for that would indicate you are boring and need to do something about it.

- Start talking and watch people's eyes. If they drop to the floor and stay there, that's not good. Next, watch their feet. If they start moving away, that's another clue.
- Look back at the number of parties you've been invited to over the last ten years. If they were all at your house, I think you know what that means.
- If you're making a presentation at work, count the number of yawns while you're talking. If the yawners are not even covering their mouths, you have a serious problem.
- When you go into a florist shop, do the plants wilt?
- Have you been recommended as a potential cure for insomnia?

- How exciting is your wardrobe? When you go to the library, are you the same colour as the walls? Not good.
- What kind of car do you drive? A '64 Rambler doesn't make you a playboy. Even with the reclining seats.
- What kind of movies do you talk about? If it's a musical or a Disney—or, even worse, a Disney musical—you've just become the Bermuda Triangle of movie talk.
- Which entrée do you order at a restaurant? Paella or pad thai are okay. A grilled cheese sandwich with skim milk is a fist magnet.
- What tunes do you have on your iPod? Barry Manilow, Johnny Mathis and Yanni are the Axis of Ennui. You have no chance.

If more than five of the above apply to you, you must change or become fiercely independent.

QUICK TIP #10: SLIPPERY STAIRS

At bedtime, bring your kid into the kitchen and hand him a glass filled all the way to the brim with soda pop. Tell him he can't drink it until he's up in his room. Within a week, those stairs will no longer be slippery.

ANOTHER PAUSE FOR THOUGHTS

If you need proof that your actions today will affect your life tomorrow, eat a pound of cheese.

If you can't say anything good about anybody, you will probably get your own TV series.

When you shirk a responsibility, some of the energy you saved must be directed at coming up with a really good excuse.

If you can't impress women with your body or your mind, you will have to buy them things.

It's okay to think of something without saying it.

Wait until people ask to see your scar.

There is no tattoo that helps a person get a job.

Animals can smell fear, but fortunately, people can smell animals.

Women with large breasts are generally more successful than men with large breasts.

Proctologists aren't good at looking people in the eye.

Not everybody is against income tax—just the people who pay it.

Sex is great, but it's usually a poor career choice.

You may be quick on your feet, but you can't outrun even the smallest explosion.

Your dog being your best friend may be mostly due to a lack of alternatives for each of you.

Beginnings are exciting. Endings are satisfying. It's the stuff in the middle that makes you what you are.

Ignorance is no excuse, but there is something endearing about mind-numbing stupidity.

A QUIET PLACE

In the old days, men would either find or create a place where they could go to be alone and think or meditate or reflect or just stare blankly. Maybe it was one of the outbuildings on the farm or a secluded spot in the woods, but it was a place they could always go when they need a little "me" time. And now that the forces of justice and equality have rightfully come into play, everyone is basically a man. That means that all members of the family would benefit from having a quiet place they can go when they really need to be alone.

If you're one of the fortunate few whose house was built in the '50s by a pessimist, you will have a bomb shelter in the backyard. It is so easy to convert a bomb shelter into a *calm* shelter. It already has the privacy, soundproofing and ability to store large amounts of alcohol that are major components in any stress-relief exercise. The rest of us will need to find a way to build or convert some space on our property to suit the purpose. It's better if it's not part of the house. No matter how secluded or secure you make any room in your house, the presence of other people in your environment will always mean there's the possibility your space will be invaded, like that time the lock let go on the bathroom door. Also, there's a psychological benefit to leaving the house and entering another structure and, by inference, another world. But before you can choose what to do next, you need to look at the desired properties of the completed structure.

No Windows. You're not there to look out. If you do, you may see things in your yard that bring twinges of regret or guilt. And remember, if you can see the cops, they can see you.

Soundproofing. This has to be state-of-the-art, two-way soundproofing. You don't want to hear the outside world, and for sure you don't want the outside world to hear you. The stress-relief process often includes very loud one-way conversations between you and imaginary people who don't see things your way.

Climate control. If it gets very cold, you'll have to wear too many clothes to be able to relax. It's also difficult to open a beer can with your gloves on. If it gets too hot, you will take your clothes off, and that has rarely worked to your advantage.

Entertainment centre. A wall-sized high-def TV and a large wooden crate full of spare batteries for the remote.

Restricted access. One door—reinforced with a dead bolt on the inside. Line the walls with foil to prevent cellular signals from getting in or out. You are only there to communicate with yourself, and that's a local call.

If you have enough property and a good relationship with the building permit guy, you can maybe build some kind of a bunker out behind the compost heap. Otherwise, you're looking at a garage conversion. If you want to be able to keep using the garage as a garage, you can maybe enclose the attic portion and have your hideaway up there, but in my experience, when you feel like hunkering down, you want to descend, not ascend (and certainly not ass end), so I suggest you jack up the garage, build a basement under it and then drop it back down. Cut a trap door in the floor of the garage, slide a stepladder down it, and you've got yourself a bunker.

Route the exhaust from the car out through the garage door so you can have the car running. Set the car's automatic climate control for 72 degrees Fahrenheit, then run a length of dryer hose from the car fan down into the bunker. Just be sure not to put too many supplies in there or you may never want to go back to the house. To be fair to all, you need to offer use of the space to everyone in your family. You can even set up a schedule so that everybody gets equal time. My guess is that after a week or two, it'll be all yours.

THE DANGERS OF POINTING A FINGER

I'm sure you all know that old chestnut that when you point a finger, three of your fingers are pointing at yourself. Well, I think I can prove it.

My friends and I have been going to the same restaurant for years, but lately there've been a few problems. It all started when the restaurant owner did a renovation. There were a lot of food stains on the walls, so he put in new panelling; and many of the deer heads were starting to moult, so he had them urethaned. The floor was looking pretty rough, too, so he installed light dimmers. Well, ever since, he's been getting lots of complaints from the regulars that he's screwed up the acoustics and ruined the lighting. They're saying it's so loud they can't hear themselves think and the dimmers make it so dark they can't see what they're eating.

Let me deal with those problems one at a time. For most of my friends, not being able to hear what they're thinking is not necessarily the restaurant's fault, or even a bad thing. Most of the time, if they could hear themselves think it would be the sounds of silence. Secondly, I've been hearing what they're thinking for the last forty years and it would be nice to take a break. In the same way, not being able to see what you're eating can be a blessing, particularly in this restaurant.

But these are my friends and I feel like I should take their complaints seriously, so I went to the restaurant early and just kind of sat back and took notes as the evening unfolded. I watched a bunch of people arrive to have dinner. Lots of young people on dinner dates, a few middle-aged couples and even fewer old guys like me and their wives. Generally, the young people could talk to each other easily and there didn't seem to be any acoustic problems. Even the middle-aged folks seemed to be okay with whatever audio challenges they were facing. But once the old guys got there, they were having trouble hearing what the others were saying. Their solution was to raise their voices, which upped the overall noise level of the restaurant. Now the other customers were having trouble hearing, so they started yelling. That just made the old folks take it up a notch, and pretty soon it sounded like a football game in there.

Same deal on the lighting. The young and middle-aged customers were having no problem reading the menu or seeing what they were eating. It was only the old, crotchety folks like me who were holding the menus at arm's length or taking them to the restroom to read.

So here's the lesson: It is not automatically the responsibility of the restaurant owner to make up for my hearing loss and diminished vision. Maybe the restaurant doesn't have a problem at all until guys like me go there. Maybe if I explain it like that to my wife, we can just stay home and order a pizza. How do you like my chances?

HOW TO ADJUST TO GLOBAL WARMING

I know we get a lot of mixed messages about global warming. If Al Gore is so convinced it's happening, why has he packed on all that extra insulation? And how come the record-breaking hottest temperatures took place sixty or seventy years ago? And how come it's July and I'm wearing a sweater?

But we amateur idiots have to put our opinions aside and instead listen to the opinions of the professional idiots. For us, being an idiot is just a hobby; these guys do it for a living. So I guess the mature thing to do is to accept that global warming is a real issue and we need to take action to mitigate the impact and we know we're going to do that. But there are other ramifications to global warming, and we need to prepare for them. Our lives are gradually going to change forever, and we need to adjust our lifestyles accordingly. Here are a few suggestions that will help you adapt and eventually embrace global warming.

Reassign your snow blower. It will now become a manure spreader. Rev it up full and walk it into your compost heap while spinning the discharge cowling so that the fertilizer gets spread evenly throughout the garden. Just make sure it's not a windy day and learn to keep your mouth shut (never a bad tip).

Recycle. Take that obsolete skiing and hockey equipment and build yourself an eye-catching fence.

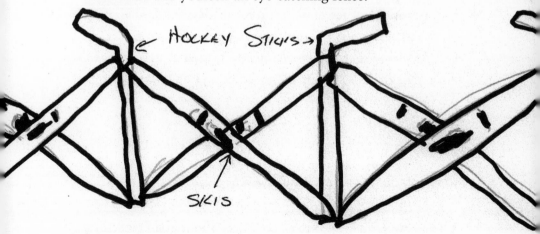

Get cooking. Take the block heater out of your car and install it through the drain hole of a clay flowerpot. Fill it with chunks of beef and vegetables and add water. Then just plug it in and let it stew all day. (You're probably used to that.) Anybody can have a crock pot; you've just made a *block* pot. It's absolutely free and worth every penny.

Frothy the Showman. Stuff your snowmobile suit with all your old scarves and mitts. Let the kids jam a carrot into his helmet, and winter's darn near as much fun as it ever was.

A taste of history. Fill your laundry tub with pork and cod and then dump bags of road salt over top. By the time the salt dissolves and evaporates, the pork and cod will be cured so that you can store them for another time when you have a weak moment. The only downside is the laundry tub will now be a small mound of rusty metal.

In the still of the night. Boil your antifreeze to concentrate the alcohol, then use it to make an exotic tropical punch. I would suggest "family hold back" on this one. Maybe it's more of a table decoration than an actual beverage. I suppose you could serve it to people you don't expect to see again, because chances are, you won't.

You scratch mine. An ice scraper makes a dandy backscratcher. Especially for the spot up between your shoulder blades that you can never reach. If your itch is lower, I suggest you go with a snow shovel. It's got a longer handle and the wide blade will accommodate even the biggest butt.

Secure bird feeder. With no winter to kill your battery, you're not going to need those jumper cables anymore, so why not use them to give the birds a safe place to come for a snack? Attach each end to an old battery and carefully remove the insulation every foot or so. The bird feeder will hang from insulated wire. If a squirrel tries to steal the food by doing the tightrope-walking trick, every foot or so he'll get an electrical reminder that he is not welcome at this particular restaurant.

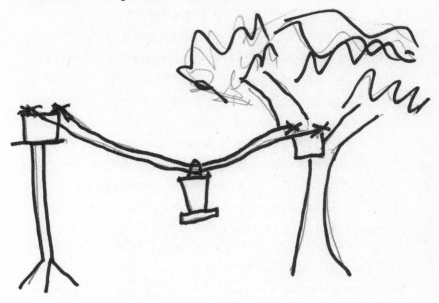

BEWARE OF GOLF

A lot of guys my age have taken up golf. That's because when you get to a certain point in your life where you've either done what you set out to do or you've given up on the possibility of things getting better, you start looking around for something to do that will fill in your spare time and give you a challenge and maybe even lead to some new friendships. These guys think that golf is the answer. They are so wrong and here's why.

- Nobody who plays golf is ever happy with their game.
- No matter how well you play, you know you could have played better.
- Right after you make fun of somebody who throws their clubs, you will throw your clubs.

- When you start playing, you'll be horrible, then you'll get better, then you'll be horrible again. That pattern will continue until you quit the game.
- Golf makes you miserable, and it's so expensive you won't be able to afford to do anything fun.
- No matter how good you get at certain areas of the game, you will be completely focused on the part you do worst.
- Golf could be compared to a dental appointment, if dental appointments were four hours long.
- Golf will remind you how little you think of yourself.
- Golf was invented in Scotland so that the whole world could be as miserable as the Scots are.
- The longer you play golf, the more swear words you'll need.
- It's the only sport where the best players in the world aren't all that good at it.
- Golf won't kill you, but it will make you think about it.

DON'T PLAY TOO MUCH SOLITAIRE

As I've mentioned elsewhere in this book, many men have a natural tendency to want to do things on their own. Left unchecked, some of these men will ultimately be spending over 80 per cent of their time alone. Some of you who are reading this are thinking, "I don't see a problem." But that *is* the problem. The deterioration that comes from being alone too much is subtle, yet severe. Don't let it happen to you. Here are a few of the warning signals that you should watch for to make you're not spending too much time on your own.

- Lack of conflicting opinions has convinced you that you are pretty much right about everything.
- You think THAT shirt goes fine with THOSE pants.

- You consider yourself an above-average singer.
- You are totally convinced that function overrules form, even with your haircut.
- You reminisce about uncomfortable conversations from your past and then say what you should have said. Out loud.
- People have stopped coming to the garage to see if you're all right.
- You watch television seventeen hours a day, even though you're only awake for twelve of them.
- You catch a mouse in your pantry and make a concerted effort to befriend him.
- You take your pants off when gardening.
- You believe that everything good that's happened to you has been from your superior intelligence and skill, while everything bad has just been rotten luck.
- You hide from the mailman in case he accidentally says something annoying—like "Good morning."
- You record JEOPARDY! and keep watching it until you get all the answers—in the form of a question—right.
- You have several plaques and trophies that you made for yourself.
- You've decided that you have nothing to apologize for, and even if you did, it would be too late now.
- You know all of the things that are wrong with the world and none of them can be traced back to you.
- If it turns out your wife was right all these years, you're going to be really, really upset.

FRIENDS WITH BENEFITS

It is very common that over the years a man will build up a special relationship with one particular guy—a guy he would describe as his best friend. It happens most often when both of the men stay in one place, particularly if that one place is a small town where neither of them has many alternatives.

There's a downside to these relationships. Sure, he's your best friend, but sometimes he is unable to supply what you need when you need it. It's at times like these you need to have "friends with benefits," where neither of you is looking for a serious, committed relationship. This is casual and occasional, but hey, as long as nobody gets hurt, there shouldn't be a problem.

But if you're thinking of trying something like this, you need to know there are a few ground rules. You have to be completely honest with the new guy. Let him know from the get-go that you are not looking for a new best friend. It's just that from time to time your best friend falls short of your needs. And if this new guy can accept that and is prepared to have a friends-with-benefits relationship, it could be a good thing for everybody. It will relieve stress for you and the new guy, and will ease the pressure on your best friend to be continually at your service. He no longer is the only one you can call when you need to borrow a power tool or when you need help getting a cow out of your trunk or when you need a ride to court. You've got the new guy to fill that role once in a while.

The tricky part is to keep it casual. Having the new guy help you change a tire is part of the normal give-and-take of a friends-with-benefits scenario. But bringing him up to the cottage for a three-day sleepover while you build a bunkie together is sending a message that is only going to cause problems. You're saying this has gone beyond casual and the new guy is coming dangerously close to becoming your new best friend. You need to pull back immediately or you could lose your current best friend, and that would be a horrible mistake. Best friends are not as hard to find as friends with benefits are. As any married guy will tell you, it's the casual stuff that's damn near impossible to pull off.

HOW TO PREPARE FOR THE BIG DAY

As we get older, it gets more and more difficult to prepare our minds and bodies for any major challenge. The key is to adjust for the ravages of age by allowing much more prep time in your schedule, because you're going to need it.

The physical side is the easy one, so let's start there. You need to start taking walks—not necessarily long walks, but walks with lots of twists and turns and complete 180-degree changes in direction. Start with five minutes a day and then gradually build that up to six minutes a day.

Next, you can work on your flexibility (I don't mean the ability to accept a different point of view—I'm sure you've given up on that one—I'm taking about your joints). If you can still bend your knees, do it. If not, try falling over and then see how fast you can get up. Same thing with the elbows. You need to build the strength and flexibility in your arms, so try having four large drafts instead of six small ones.

You'll need to tone up your back muscles, so try sitting on a chair and bouncing a twenty-five-pound turkey up and down on one leg. If you do it where the neighbours can see, it will prevent them from coming over for Thanksgiving dinner.

The only other physical component you need to work on is the ability to function without your usual fourteen hours of sleep a day. Try setting the clock radio to 4 A.M., tuned to a hip-hop station at full volume. That will not only limit your sleep, it will be a test of whether you can wake up in a good mood under any circumstances.

We have now moved into the mental area. This is the most important aspect of preparing for any difficult experience. You need to build your mental toughness. Get your wife to yell at you every half-hour or so. If she already does this, you have a huge advantage. Next, stop making commitments to anything. Record your favourite shows while you're watching them, in case you get called away or distracted. Turn down all invitations—you might drop by, you might not. Work on your alertness (your wife will back me on that one). Practise napping with one eye open. Hint: You can use a toothpick, but a Q-tip is safer.

Replace the word *yes* in your vocabulary with "we'll see." This signifies that you're adjusting to the fact that during this adventure, your time and your activities will be largely out of your control. Similarly, you must free up your financial resources to make them available, as you must be able to effortlessly spend unlimited funds without guilt or you're in for a rough time.

When you've done all of the above and you feel you're ready physically, mentally and financially, take a deep breath, phone your son or daughter and say okay, you're now ready to take the grandchildren for the weekend.

QUICK TIP #11:
GETTING FARTHER
ON EMPTY

Your car's gas line runs from the bottom edge of the front of your gas tank, so you can get farther on empty if the back of the car is higher than the front. You can do that in three ways: by only driving downhill, by flattening the front tires, or the ultimate, by only driving downhill after flattening the front tires.

POWER PAINT

If you're like me, you probably take a lot of grief from the neighbours because your house needs painting and there's a useless junk car sitting on the front lawn. Well, here's a plan that will allow you to kill two birds with one stone, assuming killing birds with stones is legal in your area.

When people don't get around to doing things like painting their homes, 90 per cent of the time it's not the cost of the materials, it's the amount of work required. The other 10 per cent of the time, it's both. The only other possible reason a man doesn't paint his house is because he's not married.

The solution I'm presenting here takes almost all of the time and work out of the job, so all you're left with is the cost of the paint. And because the job gets done so quickly, you'll have ample time to recoup the money spent through gainful employment—or returning your empties.

For you to grasp the scientific principles behind this technique, you need to have a basic understanding of the operating procedure of an internal combustion engine. As the piston descends, it creates a vacuum inside the combustion chamber so that when the intake valve opens, fuel is sucked in.

The valve closes as the piston comes back up, compressing the fuel-and-air mixture.

When the piston gets to the top, the spark plug fires and the resultant explosion drives the piston back down.

This time, as the piston returns, the exhaust valve opens, letting the exhaust gases escape and kill the rainforest.

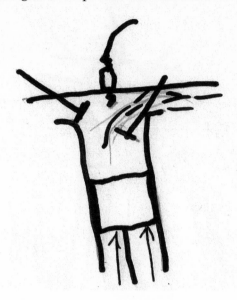

This cycle repeats for every cylinder. Let's say your old junker has a six-cylinder engine. It really doesn't need all six to run, so we're going to run it on five cylinders as described above. That's because we want to convert the sixth cylinder into a paint sprayer. It's easy. If the car is fuel injected, remove the fuel line from the sixth cylinder and drop the loose end into the can of paint. If it has the old-style carburetor and intake manifold, you'll need a way to isolate the intake port for that cylinder and then run a hose from that port into the can of paint, using an adapter made out of non-flammable duct tape—if such a thing is ever invented. Next, remove the spark plug and replace it with a three-inch nipple. You don't have to use a nipple, but a nipple works best and besides, it's fun saying "nipple." Attach a garden hose to the other end of the nipple. (I promise that's the last time I'll say "nipple." Other than that "nipple." And *that* one.)

In this configuration (see diagram on next page), when you start the engine using the other five cylinders, as the piston of the sixth cylinder goes down it will suck the paint into the combustion

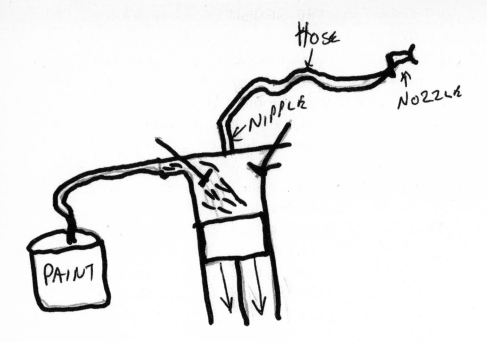

chamber and then expel it through the garden hose on compression. Any residue will be forced out the exhaust valve and extend the life of your muffler by painting the inside of it. You shouldn't get any overspray out through the exhaust pipe, but just in case, I suggest you don't paint the house while wearing your good pants.

Use a garden hose spray nozzle to aim the paint, using the wide fan spray for the large areas and the narrow stream for the fine work like window trim or lattice or changing a sign saying CONDEMNED to CONDONED. And check your spelling—CONDOMED is a whole different word.

Cleanup is just as quick and easy. Take the intake hose out of the paint and drop it into a can of turpentine. Then just spray until the hose is clear. Try to keep the turpentine spray well away from the barbecue grill.

And you're done. You've made your house look better and you've given an old car a purpose. Your neighbours will be so impressed, they'll want you to paint *their* houses. And if it was a windy day, you already did.

RESPECTING THE SENSITIVE HANDYMAN

I'm guessing you have a handyman in your house who's been more or less fixing and building things for most of your adult life. And what happens over time is that you tend to take that person for granted and begin to get more and more critical of the quality of their workmanship. You need to remember that handymen have feelings too. Some of the things you say in the spirit of being constructive are in fact hurtful. From the handyman's perspective, he's giving his time and best efforts to make life better for everyone in the family, and when these are not appreciated, he can have thoughts of going postal. So before that happens in your house, here are a few examples of what not to say to your handyman as he shows you the results of his latest project.

- Oh boy . . .
- Is it finished?
- What's that thing sticking out on the side there?
- Shouldn't it be level?
- Is the duct tape just on there until the glue dries?
- What exactly IS that?
- I hope it didn't cost anything.
- You'll need to take it all apart before garbage day.
- Did you hurt yourself again?
- It doesn't look anything like the one in the magazine.
- I blame myself.
- Don't let the neighbours see it.
- Which way am I supposed to look at it?
- Is this what you've been doing all day?
- We should check our insurance coverage before anybody sits on that.
- You get the gasoline, I'll get the matches.

THE REAL IRONMAN TRIATHLON

For years now, there's been this incredible athletic event called the Ironman Triathlon where a bunch of guys swim like a hundred miles, bicycle a hundred more and then relax by running the last hundred. You get an award just for finishing, and if you actually win the triathlon, you're like a god. Well, I think that's great and I have a lot of respect for anyone who would put that much work and dedication into training for the event and then actually be able to succeed at it. But I don't think we should get too carried away with its significance or even assume that this definition makes you greater than you really are. So I've come up with a different version of the same contest. This is what I call the *Real* Ironman Triathlon, and there's no difference between being first and last. If you finish, you win. If you don't, you don't. Here are the events.

EVENT ONE: Puberty
The goal here is to survive your body growing at an uncontrollable rate at the same time as you're dealing with body odour and random hair gain, not to mention your voice cracking while you ask the doctor about your pimples. And while all that's going on you feel a desperate need to be attractive to girls. Good luck with that one. And as the hormones rage, you're expected to excel in athletics and academics and have a clear enough mind to choose a career path. No wonder most teenagers get their noses pierced. That may be the most fun of the year.

EVENT TWO: Courtship and Marriage
Surviving the randomness of finding a compatible mate—an occurrence a lot like planets from different galaxies having intersecting orbits at exactly the right moment—you get married and start a family while simultaneously attempting to launch a career. You struggle through diapers and preschool and the teen years

and college and eventually see them leave the nest. And the job requires more time than the kids, so you don't really give enough of it to either, but you're hoping that neither notices. They do. Financial setbacks and personal problems continue, but the true Ironman continues to find a way to move forward.

EVENT THREE: Retirement and Fogeyhood

This is the most challenging of the three stages, because now you're having to deal with the results of all of the decisions you made in the first two. Maybe if you'd been a better parent, the kids wouldn't still be living with you. Maybe if you'd been a better employee, they wouldn't have cut you loose five years early. Maybe if you'd been a better husband, you wouldn't be alone surfing the Internet. But if you can get through this final stage with a wife and a family and maybe even a grandchild or two, then you, sir, are a *Real* Ironman. Take a bow, because that is the second-greatest honour a person can achieve. The greatest honour is being an Iron*woman*, because that includes all of the above plus childbirth.

IN LOVING MEMORY OF THE TWO-CYCLE ENGINE

At this time, the two-cycle engine is still with us, but the writing is on the wall. The levels of pollution going into our air and water will surely soon seize them up once and for all. And when that happens, all men everywhere need to bow their heads and give a small prayer of thanks to the passing of an icon. I suggest you rip this out of the book and keep it in your wallet so you'll have it ready when that day arrives.

> *Here's to you, my blue-smoke friend*
> *Hard to start, but once we got you going, you would*
> *run all day and into the night*

The weed whacker, the chainsaw, the leaf blower, the
   snowmobile, the outboard, you were always there
   for us
Never again will I need to mix oil with the gas
Never again will I come home smelling like Kuwait
I will miss your whine—it was a cheap whine and I
   drank my fill
You helped me clear the brush behind my house
You helped me trim the driveway
You helped me get rid of that finger I apparently didn't
   need
Still, you never quit on me
You often wouldn't go at all, but when you did, you
   never quit
You proved to me that you can have a heart, even if you
   don't have valves
You will be missed
I haven't seen anything so light that could spin so fast —
Maybe once in a strip joint, but I digress —
For years, they tried to replace you with electric motors,
   but we all knew better
They didn't have the power you had
They didn't have power at all once we ran over the
   extension cord
So I raise my glass here and salute you, old friend
Thank you, my smoky little helper
I'd ask for two minutes' silence, but that was more than
   you ever gave us

Amen.

TRANSLATING SAILOR TALK

I'm not really sure how it all began, but for centuries sailors have had a whole different language that they use to refer to aspects of boats and boating. A kitchen on a boat is called a galley. Why? What's wrong with the word *kitchen*? Why do we have to learn a whole new word for something we all understand? It's all just part of the mystery of being a sailor. So I thought it would be helpful to at least start a translation chart that would help normal people understand what the heck sailors are talking about.

WORDS
galley = kitchen
head = toilet
sore head = leaning over the toilet
sheet = rope
rope = line
line = Would you like to see my dinghy?
rode = anchor chain
rowed = ran out of gas
starboard = right
port = left
bow = front
stern = rear
starboard bow = right ahead
port astern = left behind
calm = man overboard
mayday = woman overboard
galleon = Spanish warship
gallon = daily rum ration
arrrgggh = right on
gunwhale (pronounced *gunnel*) = edge of the deck
tunwhale = something you ride a small boat through (e.g., Tunwhale of Love)

PHRASES

Shiver me timbers = My legs are cold

Ahoy there, Matey = Yo mama

Reef the jib = Smoke pot

Trim your main = Put that back in your pants

Hard to lee = Turn, you idiot!

Preparing to come about = Getting ready to vomit

Heeling on a broad reach = Dancing with a trashy woman

Heaving to windward = Making chili

Hoisting the spinnaker = Taking Viagra

Being keelhauled = Going to a proctologist

Batten the hatches = There's a bat in the hatches

Swabbing the deck = DNA testing of playing cards

Red skies at night = I have wine in my eye

OLD-GUY PRACTICE

None of us is getting any younger, and you don't want to have any problems adjusting to old age, so I suggest you practise being an old guy now. That way, when the time comes, you'll be ready.

- Drive in the passing lane at half the speed limit with your turn signal on.
- Slump down in the driver's seat so your noggin is completely hidden by the headrest.
- Dawdle aimlessly through the mall with your mouth open.
- Try to work your bowel movements into every conversation.
- Hike up your pants half an inch every six months. You may start to notice chafing in your armpits, but you will eventually build up calluses.

- Approach strangers randomly and tell them what they're doing wrong.
- Turn that smile upside down.
- Walk with the fluidity and grace of a stepladder.
- Park your car by ear.
- Ride a charter bus to Branson, Missouri, and sit near the restroom.
- Explain how everything used to be so much better.
- See how loud the TV can go.
- Wear huge sunglasses.
- Shave your legs.
- Use the time it takes you to get out of a recliner to time an egg.
- Fall asleep during a porno movie.
- Have your pharmacist on speed dial.
- Don't eat anything that has flavour.

ANIMAL DEFENCE

For anyone who spends a lot of time outdoors, whether by choice or a restraining order, the time will eventually come when you are confronted by a hostile animal. The way you respond when this happens can be the difference between life and death— or can at the very least allow you to keep all of your toes. As in other challenges—like, say, the honeymoon night—the secret is preparation and practice. Long before you get into a confrontational situation with a wild animal, you need a realistic assessment of all of your feasible options. Generally, you have three: try to escape, stay and fight, and the ever-popular stand perfectly still and do nothing.

In the following analysis, I'm going to assume you're a typical middle-aged man whose greatest sports achievement involved eating. Let's start by identifying the types of animals you'd be capable of escaping from:

Animals you can outrun: turtles, snails, hippos and moss
Animals you can outclimb: horses, rhinos, hamsters and fish
Animals you can outjump: elephants, pigs, caterpillars and manatee
Animals that can catch and hurt you: all others

So if escape is not an option, let's evaluate your chances if you stay and fight:

Animals that have smaller teeth than you: salamanders, trout, chipmunks and flies (either kind)
Animals that have fewer teeth than you: leeches
Animals that are weaker than you: n/a
Animals that are less fierce than you: butterflies
Animals that will fight and hurt you: all others

That brings us to your best option: stand perfectly still and do nothing. It may sound cowardly, but there are several advantages to using this approach when defending yourself against any animal.

- The animal will not see you as a threat, so his level of aggression will decrease, causing him to rip off only one of your legs.
- The animal will move away because he finds you pathetic, especially if you wet yourself.
- It will give you an opportunity to finally welcome God into your life.
- The animal will get a chance to smell you and rethink his plan of eating you.
- The ultimate carnage will be localized, making a lot less work for the cleanup crew.

Of course, the best defence against an animal attack is to have a friend with you who is actually slower and weaker than you are—someone you can turn to and say, "Just stand perfectly still and do nothing while I go for help." If you can't find anyone slower and weaker than you, you should move to the city.

HOW TO BUILD YOUR OWN AIRPLANE

As is true with most things in life, there are different levels of proficiency within any specific category. Just because a guy can build a picnic table doesn't mean he could make a watch. There are many factors that come into play—precision, patience, sobriety, etc.—and the qualifications get even more stringent when building something that could, if built improperly, lead to personal injury and death.

It's also true when making certain types of repairs, like replacing key components on a car or a nuclear device. So when a handyman evolves to the point where he decides to build, and then fly, his own airplane, he must be prepared to max out his skill level and working tolerances. If any of you are thinking of doing something along that line, here are a few simple tips that can help you decide whether or not you should try to fly in something you built in your garage.

- Don't.
- Check your tools. You can't cut and drill to five one-thousandths of an inch with a handheld cordless drill and a hacksaw. Similarly, duct tape is a repair device, not a construction tool.
- Check your eyesight. The fit may look good enough to you, but if you have to squint to read a billboard, there's a 50/50 chance that you've put the wing on upside down.

- Use the right materials. If the instructions call for aluminum, that's what you need to get. Don't use steel plate or plywood just to save a few bucks.
- Use all the parts. If they say the tail needs to be attached using all ten bolts, do it. It may seem like overkill to you right now, but you don't want it to cross your mind at five thousand feet. Chances are you'll have other things to think about.
- Be fussy about the engine. It's very important that the engine either runs perfectly or not at all.
- When you get about a third of the way into the project, take a break and rethink the whole thing. Drop an egg onto a concrete floor and try to imagine what that must feel like.
- Move the beer fridge so it's at least five hundred yards from the construction zone.
- Make sure all wing flap and rudder cables are tight, without any play. All work and no play makes a safer airplane.
- Do regular visual inspections. Stand back and look at the overall project every few days. If it doesn't look like an airplane, it isn't.
- Don't skimp on the tires. Get the largest, softest ones available. A plane crash is a disaster—a plane BOUNCE is usually quite amusing.
- When the airplane is complete and ready for its first flight, hire a test pilot. If he inspects the plane and turns down the job, don't second-guess him. If he inspects the plane and accepts the job, rescind the offer and go yourself. No point in wasting money.
- Before taking off on your maiden voyage, make sure your life insurance is paid up, say goodbye to everyone and drop photo ID into your underwear so they can identify the body.

HOW TO GET OFF THE GRID

With the current concerns over the environment and pollution and the creation of greenhouse gases, many people are interested in "getting off the grid"—which means living in such a way that they don't consume extra energy and thus leave a minimal carbon footprint. They want to be known as "green" people. Taken to its extreme, there are many advantages to getting off the grid, including the financial savings of never having energy, food or water bills. It requires a little creativity and a willingness to think outside the box, so naturally I'm one of the first people you'd come to. Let's start with the basics.

PROPERTY

You have a small piece of land that you either purchased or won in a poker game or claimed through squatter's rights after you squatted on it and then couldn't stand up. In any case, your goal is to live on this property in a self-sufficient way. The first step is to determine the wind direction, as made famous in the old expression, "See which way the wind blows." You can determine prevailing wind direction by purchasing a wind vane or simply by spending a day at a nearby pig farm. Once you've established that, the upwind side of your property will be your front lawn and the opposite side will be your septic bed.

HOUSING

Build your house between the front and back yards, starting with four scrap school buses. These will be the walls of your home. A standard exterior brick

wall with insulated studs has an R-value of 40, but a full-size school bus with the wheels off and the windows up has an R-75 rating. Position one of the school buses as shown so that you can enter the house through the rear emergency exit and leave through the folding door.

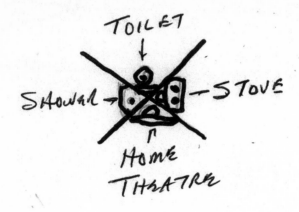

Pace off the floor to determine the exact centre of the interior space. Put a big X there, as this will be the hub of your home. Mark off four spokes to each of the four corners of the school bus walls. These four spaces will contain the stove, the sink/shower/bidet/drinking fountain, the toilet and the home theatre.

HEAT

The stove will burn things commuters throw out of their cars on the highway. If someone has abandoned a boat, you are allowed to burn it, but be sure it's wood. Burning fibreglass will get you off the grid in ways you didn't want. The toilet will be hooked up to the septic bed out the back. To provide fresh water, you'll need a large swing set from a local park, which you'll be borrowing on a permanent basis. Mount it inside the home and upside down as shown.

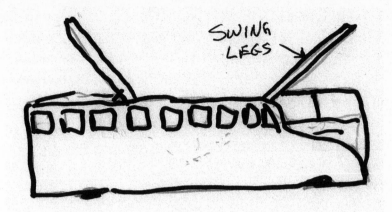

WATER

Now take a large metal shed with a conventional pitched roof and invert it so it rests between the legs of the swing. Don't let the thought of legs in the air cause you to lose focus—this is important work. Cut a hole in the join of the inverted roof and mount a large storage tank under it. The shed is now a huge funnel that will gather rain water and snow to give you an unending supply of drinking water that will not only keep you nourished, it will also challenge your immune system. Route some of this water through the stove to heat it. Now you have hot water for washing yourself.

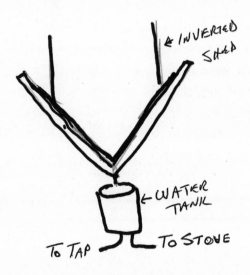

ELECTRICITY

Power the home theatre with rechargeable batteries hooked up to a charger. Recharge the batteries in the middle of the night by running an extension cord from the charger to your neighbour's external power outlet, as described in "How Your Pool Can Shovel Snow." Just be sure to unplug it before he gets up.

FOOD

You can grow your own if you're a purist, but there's another source of food that's a lot easier and more plentiful: leftovers. Not yours—your neighbours'. In this crazy, yuppified world of ours, there are thousands of people who refuse to eat leftovers. Luckily, you're not one of them. If you feel awkward about asking your neighbours for their leftovers, tell them you're collecting food for the local mission. The government will never let you give leftovers to the underprivileged, so you'll just have to eat them yourself.

CLOTHING

Similarly, hand-me-downs are a great source of clothing. Go to the local Catholic church and make friends with tall newlyweds. Odds are they're going to have lots of kids, and they're all going to grow out of things really fast. It will be a fashion goldmine.

QUICK TIP #12: CAN YOU DRINK THE WATER?

Can you see through it? Can you smell it? Is it a funny colour?
Is it flammable? If it passes those tests, drink half a glass and
wait ten minutes. If you're still conscious and not sitting in a
restroom, the water's fine.

HOW TO MANAGE FIRE

Fire is a huge part of our lives. For most of us, it cooks our meals, heats our homes, runs our cars, provides our electricity—it can even run a refrigerator. Maybe that's why we've always had such a fascination with fire. We have campfires and fireplaces and candles and torches. We stand and watch cars or buildings on fire and see forest fires on television. To me, fire is like having sexual urges—you're better off to find a way to manage the situation than to pretend it doesn't exist. And I think the Catholic church will back me up on that one.

So, how do we manage fire? Well, we start by identifying the primary ingredients: the source (a spark or small flame or heat from a chemical reaction), the fuel (paper or wood or gas or whatever you've got that burns) and the enabler (oxygen—without oxygen, you've got no fire).

Let's start with the spark. You can cause sparks by hitting a piece of flint or slapping your tap shoes on a cement floor or rubbing up against a well-endowed woman's cashmere sweater. Sparks are everywhere. When your car's idling it produces about four thousand sparks a minute—and if you don't believe me, try sneezing into your carburetor with a snootful of booze and you'll find your eyebrows are history. So the first step in managing fire is to be aware of sparks.

You also need to watch for open flames. Just as trying to mask sewage odours by placing scented candles over the septic system vent will only truly control odours when the resulting explosion blows your nose off, gas stoves, furnaces and water heaters have pilot lights. Propane is heavier than air, so any gas leak will eventually end up in the basement—and right after that, so will you. Again, the key is to be aware of any open flames in your home.

Next, we have chemical fire from spilled car batteries or oil-soaked rags or those odd people who spontaneously combust. Stay away from them—they tend to be heavy smokers. Looking at fuel, it's obvious that wood and gasoline and gunpowder burn well, but almost anything will burn if the flame gets hot enough—there are no rock formations on the sun.

Now, before you start to panic about the inevitability of fire destroying life as you know it, there is some good news. Without oxygen, there can be no fire, and our recent patterns of producing monstrous clouds of carbon dioxide are almost at the point of guaranteeing that fire is something future generations will never have to deal with.

HOW TO MANAGE YOUR EXPECTATIONS

Nobody enjoys disappointment, but a lot of the time we have unrealistic expectations about what's going to happen and then, when that doesn't happen, we fall into a downward spiral of anger and frustration that leads eventually to a climb up the bell tower with some kind of automatic weapon. So to avoid all of that attention, I suggest you do a better job of managing your expectations. If you have a realistic image of probable outcomes, you'll be a happier person and will be allowed to spend your declining years outside of an institution.

And never does managing your expectations play more of a role than in the search for a mate on the Internet. Maybe you've never married, or maybe your significant other has passed away or dumped you or whatever, and now you find yourself back in the game. And it's never been easier to connect with women of all ages and from all places than on the Internet. So go ahead if you want to, but before you do, take a look at these suggestions that will help you find the right person through managing your expectations.

- A woman who's more than ten years younger than you will not get your jokes.
- A woman who is fit will cause one of you to change radically. Either you'll have to get fit or she'll have to get fat.
- If you notice that a woman is beautiful, she will notice that you are not.
- Remember the way you used to not understand women and would often say and do the wrong thing? Nothing has changed.
- Meeting you will not automatically make it her lucky day.
- Chances are her past is just as embarrassing as yours.
- Imagine being hooked up with someone who is the female version of you—same shape, same attitudes, same behaviour, same level of attractiveness. Would you be satisfied with that? You're asking her to be.
- In the games that occur between partners, the long-term successful relationships come from ties, not victories.

HOW TO OUTSMART A RACCOON

Okay, let's start from the beginning on this one. Everyone says raccoons are smart, but that isn't true. With the possible exception of Uncle Bob, every human being you've ever met is smarter than the smartest raccoon that's ever been. A raccoon can't count to ten, at least not out loud, and you can't have a meaningful conversation with a raccoon, although he may occasionally nod in a way that implies he understands and agrees with your position on protectionism and its effect on international trade. Raccoons are focused and persistent and they have fingers rather than hooves. That's it. It's not brain power. All they have going for them is determination and evolution. Logic says you should be able to outsmart them.

And you can. All you need to do is get down to their level and gain an understanding of what they want and how they go about getting it. They want food, and they'll get it the easiest way possible. Mother Nature didn't leave them out in the wild where they had to fish and hunt, because if she had, they would be extinct by now. They're not good at either fishing or hunting. What they're good at is peeling the lid off a garbage can and eating its contents. Or using your chimney as a maternity ward. A nuisance? Yes, but this is not a diabolical, super-intelligent alien invader. This is an opponent that you can thwart. And it's fun. It's fun just saying the word *thwart*. Here's how you can beat the raccoons and enjoy the process.

> Eat your dinner until it's all gone. No food scraps in the garbage means no raccoons. At the very least, just throw out the stuff you don't like to eat—like cauliflower. That'll teach 'em.
>
> Frustrate them. Make a Dutch doll arrangement of garbage cans in ever-decreasing sizes, each with a lid. Once the raccoon opens and discards six or seven garbage cans, only

to find the prize in the smallest one is a gym sock, he'll be outta there.

Pull pranks. Set rat traps in the garbage shed and balance a bucket of water over the door. Hang an umbrella on your doorknob as a reminder for you when you go to put the garbage out.

Where there's smoke, there's no raccoon. Keep a smouldering fire going in your fireplace day and night. Burn green wood or eggplant. It may make the house a little warm—and smell bad, but probably not as bad as it could.

Establish routines. Raccoons create a foraging pattern and stick to it. Every night for a month, catch a fish and then bury it in the backyard. Not *your* backyard—your neighbour's. It'll be a couple of generations before the raccoons return to your place.

Think long term. One of the Lodge members cut the bottom out of his garbage can, then put the lid on and set the whole thing on top of his well. The raccoon pulled the lid off and fell down the well. I'm not sure what happened after that, but the guy drinks bottled water now.

Leave your car door open and get yourself a ten-pound bag of potatoes. Put peanut butter and cheese on the floor in the back seat—or maybe it's already there. When you see the raccoon climb inside the car, throw the potatoes at the door to slam it. Then jump in the front seat and drive the car as far away as possible. You'll be okay until the peanut butter and cheese is gone. At that point, you'll probably want to let the raccoon out with you directly in front of him.

INTERPRETING BODY MESSAGES

Throughout our lives, our bodies are constantly sending messages to our brains so that we will be able to adapt our behaviour to allow the body to repair itself. Most of the time, our brains aren't paying attention. In fact for a male between the ages of thirteen and twenty-five, his brain isn't even in charge. But as we get older, we start to realize that we need to listen to what our bodies are telling us and we need to treat the signals as warnings. So to help with that, here are some common body messages and what they mean.

MESSAGE	MEANING
aching legs	sit down
aching back	lie down
aching side	stop laughing
aching feet	get bigger shoes
aching stomach	eat less
aching head	drink less
cramps in legs	lose weight
cramps in style	it's not working
cramps in abdomen	clear your schedule
blurred vision	clean your glasses
muffled hearing	your hat's too big
losing sense of smell	a godsend
women find you attractive	you have dementia
dry mouth	dry food
eyes watering	onion stuck in nose
burning sensation in private places	eating too-spicy food
burning sensation in public places	sitting too close to the campfire
right arm is shaking	right hand is touching paint mixer
getting sore in joints	don't go into joints
stabbing pain in forehead	light fixture is too low
water on the knee	don't kneel in the basement

MESSAGE	MEANING
it seems to rain more often	male pattern baldness
you notice foot odour	you're getting shorter
sore elbow	drink with other hand
sore knee	drink with other foot
feeling sexually aroused	just kidding

HIGH STEPPERS

O nce in a while, you have to stop and acknowledge some of the unsung discoveries in the history of handymanship. One of those has to be the stepladder. It's light. It's portable. And it's very strong. Now, there are some who say the stepladder is okay, but limited as to what it can do and that if the job is more than ten feet above the ground, you put the stepladder aside and go with an extension ladder or even scaffolding. Nothing could be farther from the truth for the creative handyman.

Let's say, for example, you've volunteered your time and effort to make the church picnic a success, but unfortunately all anyone can talk about is the lid of the grill that is now sitting on the point of the steeple. And even though you've made it clear to everyone that you had no idea the propane was turned on when you playfully hit the sparker and that the committee should be thankful that nothing was damaged in the accident other than the pastor's toupee, you now feel obligated to do everything you can to get the lid down off the roof.

But instead of going conventional with a big extension ladder or even a cherry picker, here's how you can do it safely and easily with the great stepladder. The first thing you need to do is to assess the height required to do the job. In this case, it's forty feet. For an extension ladder, you'd need a fifty- or sixty-foot ladder to give you forty feet of safe elevation. Not so with the stepladder approach. All you do is multiply the height by three-eighths. That gives you fifteen, and that is the number of eight-foot stepladders you'll need to do the job. Now, you may think it's going to be difficult to come up with fifteen eight-foot stepladders, but chances are you have fourteen neighbours with one each, plus yours, and you're there. Try borrowing a sixty-foot extension ladder and see how that goes. Start with five stepladders set up as shown here:

Now add four stepladders like this:

Use woodscrews at an angle to anchor the stepladders to the bottom row and add a couple of layers of duct tape to make the setup look more professional. Now add three more stepladders:

Add two more the same way:

And finish off with the final stepladder:

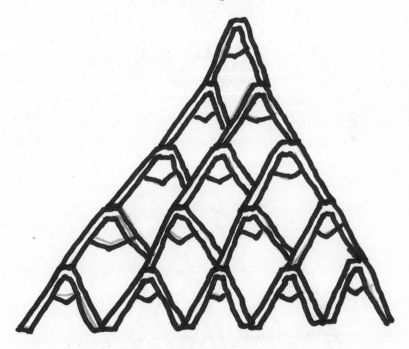

There's your forty feet of solid safe elevation, and for the first thirty-two feet of it, you can have an assistant climbing the inside stepladders and handing you whatever tools or beverages you might need. Try doing *that* with an extension ladder.

(If you actually try this, you do so at your own risk)

THE ART OF MIND READING

The ability to read another person's mind can make life so much safer and more enjoyable. For centuries, people have believed that psychic powers are something you're born with, but I say they can be learned. With just a little practice and a half-decent attention span, you too can learn how to read people's minds. Start slowly with simple, non-specific thoughts and over time you will become adept at discerning every subtle nuance of what is going on in that other person's mind. Here are a few easy lessons to get you started.

- Although the police officer says, "How are you today?" he's actually thinking about how severe the speeding ticket is going to be, based on your reaction. Anything that you say that does not involve guilt and regret will ultimately work against you.
- Although your buddy says, "Shall we have another drink?" he's thinking, "It's YOUR round."
- If something stupid just happened, your wife is thinking you're involved.
- If you have food in the house, your teenager is thinking he will eat it.
- If a salesman is trying to sell you something you don't need, he is thinking he's smarter than you. Be very careful: he could be right.
- If your boss is noticing you in any way, he's thinking he made a mistake.

- If a young woman is smiling warmly at you, she's thinking you're a friend of her dad's.
- Every representative of the tax department thinks you're lying.
- People who are being inexplicably nice to you think you have money.
- Dogs think you are tall.

You *not* thinking prevents everyone from reading your mind. Excellent work.

RARELY HEARD SENTENCES

Most conversations between people who've known each other a long time get very predictable. They'll often say the same thing in a different way, or even in the same way, over and over again. That's partly because people don't often take the time to find new things to say, and also because the same kinds of things tend to repeat themselves. As a result, there are many sentences that you've heard often throughout your life, while there are other sentences that you've almost never heard. I thought you might enjoy seeing some of those latter ones, so here's a short list of sentences you hardly ever hear.

- That's the banjo player's Porsche.
- Let's have the family Christmas dinner at our house EVERY year.
- He's a lawyer and has lots of friends.
- I'm big-boned, but mainly I'm really fat.
- I'm a qualified weatherman, and none of us have a frigging clue.
- I'm not really selling you life insurance, I'm borrowing

money from you at zero interest with no payments and the loan doesn't come due until you die.

- I don't know much about this subject, so I think I should just listen.
- I became a politician because I found it easier to get votes than a job.
- Everybody I know who buys lottery tickets has done really well.
- If there's one thing I can't stand, it's good-looking, large-breasted women.

THE GOOD SIDE OF BAD REFLEXES

When you're young and athletic—or you like to drive your car flat out all the time—there's a lot of value placed on having great reflexes. That's because a short reaction time can often make the difference when making a difficult play or applying the brakes quickly enough to avoid the radar trap.

In time, these reflexes lose their sharpness and reaction times start growing exponentially. The athlete starts getting hit in the face with the ball and the driver is spending his beer money on speeding tickets. However, for the rest of us, having really bad reflexes can be a good thing. Often in life, we respond quickly and inappropriately. A longer reaction time can save you and the rest of us from what you're thinking. Here are a few examples of the good side of bad reflexes.

When the boss announces that somebody is not pulling their weight and there are going to be cutbacks. Immediately defending yourself or jumping up and looking busy are sure signs of guilt. On the other hand, the blank stare of apathy, with an accompanying shoulder shrug followed by shuffling off to the lunch room that suggests he can't possibly be talking about *you*, will confuse him. By the time it hits you that you may be on the chopping block, you'll be into your seventh burrito and people will think you're shaking from the hot sauce.

When your wife asks if this dress makes her look fat. In the old days, that would lead to a snappy retort, followed by the sound of one person laughing, followed by the sound of one person crying, followed by the sound of one door slamming, followed by the sound of one person sleeping on the porch. Compare that to the slow turn while you try to comprehend the question. That implies that there isn't a dress in the world that could possibly make your wife look fat. The dumb look on your face sends the message that the subject of the question was the farthest thing from your mind and that not having an answer is your way of saying the question isn't worthy of an answer. You often say the nicest things by not speaking.

When you hurt yourself while others are watching. The neighbours were looking over the fence watching you build a deck, and suddenly you hurt your thumb with a hammer. Because of your poor reflexes, you have about thirty seconds before you'll feel it, so they have no idea that you've hurt yourself. Instead of giving them the satisfaction of a cruel laugh at your expense, get up slowly, wave to the neighbours with your good hand and walk calmly to the garden shed. Once inside, start up the lawn tractor to cover the sounds of your screaming.

When there's an unpleasant odour. A slow reaction is your best defence. Jumping up and waving your arms or blaming the dog isn't fooling anyone. Especially if the dog passed away a couple of years ago. Sitting calmly and being the last one to notice is your best approach. However, when you do finally notice, if you then break into fits of laughter, you will have blown your cover.

You've just done something really, really stupid. One of the fundamental elements in the illusion of innocence is calmness. If someone is frantic or trying way too hard to come up with a wacky explanation for what happened, nobody ever believes them. So here again, your inability to react quickly is your friend. It gives you an air of unforced calmness that immediately eliminates you as a suspect. Don't fight it. With any luck, by the time the finger of suspicion swings around to you, smarter minds will be well on their way to resolving the situation.

One last word of caution—although SLOW response is good, NO response is not. It is not in your best interest to exhibit continual absence of reaction to friends and family. Especially family. Especially the part of the family you're married to. Especially in the bedroom. If you get the nod in that area, that calls for a definite RSVP.

THINK HEALTHY, BE HEALTHY

The mind is a powerful thing, even in your case. They say that you become what you think about, which used to worry me when I was always thinking about girls. But now I realize that what they meant is that your thoughts determine your actions, and your actions determine your life. So, actually, your thoughts determine your life. With that in mind, I thought it might be useful to create a small sample of the kinds of thoughts you should have if you want to live long and prosper. Here are some thoughts I came up with.

- Just because I don't eat this entire extra large pizza by myself, it doesn't mean it beat me.
- Having the reputation of being "a guy who can really drink" is not as impressive as having a functioning liver.

- Even the winner in a fistfight ends up with sore hands.
- I shouldn't assume clergymen enjoy limericks.
- There is a limit to how much cheese one person should eat.
- The number of arguments I get into is directly proportional to the number of times I express my opinion.
- I should consider the feelings of anyone who is my superior—or armed.
- Roller coasters and cabbage soup are born enemies.
- It's much healthier to walk, rather than drive, to a relative's house. It's good for the cardiovascular system, and it shortens the visit.
- I need lots of sleep. The eight hours at work may not be enough.
- Everything I say and do will eventually get back to my wife.

QUICK TIP #13: SHOULD YOU BE LIFTING THIS?

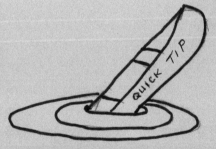

Lean against it. If it moves, it's okay for you to lift it. If it doesn't, bump heavily against it. If it moves now, it may still be okay for you to lift. If not, and you lift it anyway, lift very slowly and listen intently for any loud noise. If you hear one, and you're pretty sure it's coming out of your body, and not necessarily through an orifice, stop lifting and lie down while your wife calls 911.

A SYSTEM FOR GAMBLING

*E*ver since the first caveman said, "I'll bet you seven loincloths I can outrun that sabre-toothed tiger," people have loved to gamble. They don't think about the odds or the probability of losing; all they focus on is that somebody eventually wins and the only way they have a chance for that somebody to be *them* is if they keep playing.

Now, I'm no mathematician, so I can't tell you the exact odds on slot machines or roulette or craps or any other games of chance, but I've seen a lot of casinos and they all seem to be doing well. That has to be a clue. When you stand in a casino, note how the waitresses' outfits are more expensive than the customers' leisure suits. That's another pretty good indication as to which way the money is flowing. As a result, some gamblers prefer private poker parties on a regular night at a friend's house. That really doesn't work either because generally, with the same guys playing every week, in the long run everybody's going to come out more or less even. So without getting into the boring specifics, I suggest that one of the best gambling systems incorporates playing against strangers and having a realistic strategy of what you should do in any given situation.

So, right away, a poker tournament at a local casino would seem like a good starting point—plenty of strangers and no chance of everything evening out over time. Of course, another advantage of poker is that you're playing against people rather than mathematical odds, which is not the case with slots or roulette or craps. You can't bluff a slot machine. So, poker with strangers is a good start. The first drawback is the start-up cost of getting into a game. If you can get in with ten bucks' worth of chips, great, but these Texas hold 'em tournaments are often asking thousands of players to put up thousands of dollars, and only the top six win cash.

That may mean the risk/reward ratio is a little steep for you.

So look around and find your comfort level. No matter where that is, the most important—and most elusive—aspect of gambling isn't knowing when to step up to the table, it's knowing when to step back. If your odds of winning once are a thousand to one, your odds of winning twice are much higher. But generally, people aren't able to stop gambling, even after they've won. That's because they don't gamble to win; they gamble for the excitement they get from the *chance* of winning. That's why lotteries are so popular. For five or ten dollars a week, you have a chance of becoming a multimillionaire. It's an incredibly slim chance, but it's still a chance. I tell people they have a better probability of guessing a complete stranger's phone number than they do of winning the lottery and they respond by telling me there's no prize for guessing somebody's phone number.

People love to gamble, there's no way around it. We had a lottery at the Lodge where first prize was a million tickets to the next draw. It was very popular. So sure, playing poker with strangers at an ante level that's comfortable is a good gambling system, but the best system is to not gamble on luck at all. Instead, try investing in yourself—in a business venture or in educating yourself or in anything that makes you a more valuable person, professionally or personally. I say the best bet is to gamble on yourself. Especially if you like longshots.

REMOTE POSSIBILITIES

I find that with a lot of the technological devices they've come up with in the last few years, the unit's not powerful enough to reach its full potential. Take, for example, the garage door opener. How embarrassing and time-consuming it is for you to have to come all the way up your driveway, pressing on the remote button as you try to get into the garage before the police come around the corner. Wouldn't it be great if that remote would work from, say, half a mile away?

I can feel your smile. Well, here's how to do it. Take the remote apart and look at the circuit board. Half of the stuff is there to generate an RF signal and the other half transmits that signal through the air to the garage door sensor. You want to replace that second part, so you need to break into the circuit just before the transmitter so that you can redirect the RF signal to the input side of a 5,000-watt ham radio amplifier. You can pick up a used one pretty cheap from any wife who's tired of her husband spending every available minute down in the basement twirling knobs.

Now that you've radically boosted the signal, you'll need an upgrade on the transmitting antenna. I suggest you use an old TV aerial. You can pick them up at garage sales or in trailer parks after a tornado has gone through. Mount the antenna on a swivel bracket on your back bumper as pictured.

That way, you can use the rope to lower the antenna for bridges and tunnels.

Now you're good to go. From now on, as long as you're in sight of your garage door, you'll be able to open it. It's important that your garage door works on a different frequency than any of your neighbours', unless they're away and you need to borrow something.

The power question arises again when you sit down to watch an evening of football, baseball, basketball and hockey and the remote either doesn't work at all or is intermittent no matter how much you bang it on the arm of the recliner or take off the back and spin the batteries. It's a similar problem to the garage door opener, but it's a different technology, so it requires a different solution. The TV remote uses an IR (Infrared) signal, so an RF amplifier won't work. What you need is a military-grade laser gun. They're tricky to find. If you end up buying one on the Internet, you should use an untraceable post-office box as your address.

As you did with the garage door remote, you need to open this one up and connect from the signal-generating circuit directly into the beam accelerator on the gun. Duct-tape the trigger on the gun so it's on all the time and only activated when the remote buttons are pushed. You will now be able to change channels easily from anywhere in the room, even in full recline. Just make sure there is nobody between you and the TV, or they soon won't be. (If you're concerned about the legality of this device, it also makes an excellent gift.)

SUBJECTS YOU SHOULD NOT BRING UP WITH YOUR WIFE

It's always good to have as much communication as possible with your significant other, but, as is often the case, it's the exception that proves the rule. (I've never been quite sure what that expression means, but I've always liked the sound of it.) What I'm saying here is that no matter how easy-going, happy-go-lucky or oblivious your wife is, there are certain subjects you should never bring up. Your experience has probably shown you plenty of them, but here are a few more to add to the list:

- the SPORTS ILLUSTRATED swimsuit edition
- cooking classes
- the Mormon church
- sentences that begin with "What the hell...?"
- breast enlargement
- successful men's salaries
- Chippendales
- dress sizes
- facial hair
- lingerie
- celibacy
- arm fat
- Oprah
- erectile dysfunction
- taking too long to get ready
- grey hair
- shopping
- bad driving
- hogging the bathroom
- losing things
- household budget
- her mother
- your mother
- you

SUPPLY AND DEMAND

The law of supply and demand is one of the oldest market forces in the world, but the principle holds true in all facets of our lives. Here are a few ways to use supply and demand to help you find financial and personal success.

- If you're ugly, keep moving to smaller towns. You'll eventually look good to somebody. It's just supply and demand, with a little help from desperation.
- Don't always be sleeping on the couch when your wife comes home from work. Once in a while, be in the hammock playing hard to get.
- Point out any suspected illness to your co-workers and suggest they take a few weeks off. Your boss will soon find out you're not quite as useless as she thought.
- Hide a case of beer early at a party. Then have a midnight auction.
- If you want your teenager to ride his bike, sell the family car.
- If your guests complain about your cooking, force them to skip a couple of meals.
- If your dog is messing up the whole yard, pave it all except for a small corner.
- If your kids won't eat their vegetables, serve them as a first course. Or the ONLY course.
- Abstain from sex (as a precaution, also enroll in an anger management course).
- Go away on business for a couple of weeks. When you get home, monitor how long it is until your wife says something hurtful. Subtract an hour from that duration, and that now becomes the maximum amount of time you should spend together without taking a break from each other.
- If you're a single guy looking to get married, improve the odds by moving to a country that's at war. They won't let you be a soldier, but you'll still get to fight them off.
- Be an only child.

He's called man's best friend because he gives you uncondi-tional loyalty. But your dog can be a friend in another way—by demonstrating behavioural traits you'd be smart to copy.

If you notice you've been getting negative response from your comments or actions, maybe it's time to consult your dog to see how he would have handled the same situations. Let's start with communication.

Now, I know a bunch of you are saying, "Hey Red, dogs can't talk!" Well, first of all, this is a book, so I can't possibly hear what you're saying—and by the way, that's fine with me. Just because dogs can't talk doesn't mean they can't communicate. Watch your dog's eyes when you've done something he doesn't like. You'll see the subtle softening of focus; he may even avoid eye contact, indi-cating the sadness that comes from the way you've disappointed him, while at the same time there's a hint that he feels he has some-how failed you and this is all his fault. You'll find that if you can do the same thing, you'll get much better results than from your normal routine of angrily blaming the person you're glaring at.

On a secondary level, your dog also communicates through body language. Notice how the shoulders shrug and the head droops as he turns and walks away in shame with his tail tucked where the sun don't shine. Doesn't that pull at your heartstrings? Doesn't that get him a pat on the head and a treat at bedtime? Isn't that better than sleeping alone in the garage?

And there are lessons to be learned from normal daily occur-rences. When you arrive home, your dog rushes to greet you. You feel like he's been waiting all day for your arrival—you're special, you're his top priority. Can you imagine how great your wife would feel if you greeted her that way every time she came home? Doesn't that send a better message than hiding quietly in the basement, hoping you can watch the end of ultimate fighting before she finds you?

And when you're talking to your dog, have you ever noticed that he actually seems interested in what you're saying, even though it has no relevance to him in any way? Wow, what must that be like? When you give your dog orders and he carries them out without question, at the end of the day you feel affection for the dog and express it to him. Try doing what your wife wants without question, and the same thing could happen to you.

There are definitely valuable lessons you can learn from your dog. But like everything else in life, don't take it too far. Nobody wants to see you relieving yourself on a fire hydrant or humping your neighbour's leg.

WHAT SHE DOES NOT WANT

There has been a lot of discussion over the past few years of what it is that women want. But my male friends and I have found that to be an elusive target, so instead here is a list, based on our personal experiences, of things women *don't* want.

- Excuses
- Tropical fish
- Mining equipment
- Police at the front door
- Long-distance charges to 1-900 numbers
- T-shirts featuring profanity
- You bringing home inebriated strangers
- Hair remover as an anniversary gift
- To hold the ladder while you retrieve the barbecue lid
- Inopportune photo ops
- Any type of shovel
- Explosives
- Clothing that can't be returned

- Velvet paintings
- Wrestling memorabilia
- Monster truck season tickets
- You naked with the lights on
- Unsolicited instruction
- Lingerie that implies expectation
- Any type of broom or mop (including a Swiffer)
- To have dinner in the car
- Anything loud
- Your thumb dancing on the remote
- You asleep when you shouldn't be
- You awake when you shouldn't be

THE IMPORTANCE OF BEING IGNORANT

Knowledge is power. People who have specific areas of expertise generally have successful careers and are respected by their peers. But my point here is that ignorance is not always a bad thing. Oh sure, if you're treating a dangerous disease or disarming a nuclear device, it is handy to know what you're doing, but in the course of normal day-to-day living, it's often a great advantage not to know much—or even more importantly, to be *aware* that you don't know much. Sadly, most people who don't know much don't even know that they don't know much. But the man who's aware of his limitations always has an advantage—at work, at play and especially at home.

So let's just take a moment here to acknowledge some of the advantages to being ignorant.

- It makes you a good listener. You let the others give their opinions while you just listen and see if anything makes sense to you. This makes you very popular because guys who think they know stuff love good listeners.

- It makes you a loyal friend. You don't feel you have enough knowledge to question your buddy's decision, so instead you support it and do everything you can to help him do things his way. Friends like that are hard to find.
- It makes you unintimidating. Most people are very uncomfortable around an annoying know-it-all. They're hesitant to open their mouths for fear of being corrected and embarrassed by this guy who's an expert on everything. You don't present those restrictions. They feel they can say anything to you, and as long as it sounds even somewhat reasonable, you won't question it.
- It makes them feel important. If there's a minor crisis like a clogged toilet or there's been a small traffic accident and your van is now upside down in the living room, you will turn to someone to tell everybody what to do to correct the situation. You make them the leader and you offer yourself as a follower. People like that.
- It makes them feel smart. No matter how diplomatically a person gives you information, the underlying message is, "I know more than you do." Conversely, when you're always on the receiving end of that information, your message is, "You sure do." That person will then make the ridiculous conclusion that this somehow makes them smarter than you. That's because they confuse knowledge with intelligence. You know better, and that's why you're okay with being ignorant. In the long run, uninformed intelligence is better, than informed stupidity.

THE HANDYMAN'S PRAYER

O Heavenly Father, be with me this day,
For I am sore afraid that I will hurt myself again.
Let Thy hand guide the hammer towards the nail and
    away from my thumb.
Grant me the wisdom to wear safety glasses.
Give me the patience to measure twice and cut once—or
    measure at all.
Let the saw blade always be somewhere in the vicinity
    of the line.
Bless my drill bit with sharpness so that it will bite into
    the surface rather than dance across the countertop
    and fall into the sawdust bin with me close behind.
Let me show restraint when using my nail gun.
Give me the maturity to put screws in with a screwdriver,
    not a hammer.
Grant me the courage to change the things I can, accept
    the things I can't and the good fortune of my wife
    not realizing I can't tell the difference.
Thank you, Lord, for helping my rec room look better
    by creating dimmers.
Thank you, Lord, for safety chains and fire extinguishers.
Thank you, Lord, for all that stuff and hear us when we
    pray . . .

Our Father, who art a craftsman,
Perfectionist be thy name.
Thy power tools hum,
Thy walls are plumb,
Upstairs
As they are in the basement.
Give us this day
A utility shed,

And forgive us our borrowed tools
As we forgive those who borrow tools from us.
And lead us not into renovation,
But deliver us from moving.
For thine is the hammer
And the Skilsaw
And the duct tape,
Forever.

ABOUT THE AUTHOR

R ed Green was born up north, in the nether regions, in the
years just after the war but just before the fighting. He was
a complete surprise to his father and mother and everyone else
at the dance contest. Blessed with instinctive common sense, Red
stopped growing at the height of five foot eight, since the door to
the cabin was five foot nine. He attended Possum Lake School
until he was twenty, and then he went to junior high, which he
enjoyed very much until they assigned homework. He immediately
left school to join his father's business—collecting unemployment
insurance—but there were problems because Red didn't have
enough job skills for the government to decide what type of work
he was out of.

Eventually, Red left home to strike out on his own, which is
pretty much what he did. He tried his hand at carpentry and
welding and then, while that was healing, he tried his other hand
at plumbing and electrical work. Around this time, Red met his
wife, Bernice, at a church picnic, where they had both gone for
the free food. Red and Bernice fell instantly in love and got married later that year without even waiting for the results of the
pregnancy test. Currently, Red and Bernice are happily married
without children, living in suburbia, and maintaining a safe distance between themselves and the nearest factory outlet mall.

Red Green is the leader of Possum Lodge, Chapter 11, a northern
Ontario eyesore whose motto is *Quando Omni Flunkus Mortati*
(When All Else Fails, Play Dead). Red has the down-home wisdom

of Will Rogers, the rural charm of Garrison Keillor, and more handyman inventiveness than the entire cast of *Desperate Housewives*. Red is the glue that holds the lodge together. He is friendly, inventive, cheap and as honest as the day is long, which means he's the least honest on December 21.

When he works on his handyman projects, Red is not stupid, he's just sort of impatient. So he uses duct tape to "buy time." Red scorns fads and fancies. He cuts through the crap. He is one of a kind. Although some might just call that wishful thinking.

ABOUT THE ILLUSTRATOR

R ed Green's drawings have a uniqueness and a simplicity, combined with an implied lack of ability to go in any other than this brave direction. He writes: "I started my artistic career early, and then it was abruptly suspended when I entered Grade 4. I was twelve years old at the time. They would have put me into Grade 5, but my father was there. For the next forty-odd years, my drawing skills were only used to create maps for people I never wanted to see again, and to use as a visual aid when explaining to the cops how the car hood and both overhead valve covers ended up on the roof of the drive-in snack bar. Then, in the 1990s, I illustrated my own poetry books, which I very carefully kept hidden away until the publisher allowed me to do the illustrations for this book. If you find the drawings unclear and confusing, it will probably make you feel better to hear that they all make perfect sense to me."

ABOUT THE PHOTOGRAPHER

Red Green has found digital cameras a godsend for taking acceptable pictures at last. He says: "Features like auto-focus and backlight filter are great, but the major breakthrough has to be the delete button. On occasion, I have actually suffered a cramp in my thumb from using it to delete pictures of it. There was also a bit of a learning curve until I realized that, for auto-focus to work, the object you were taking a picture of had to be somewhere in the frame, preferably in the middle. Of course, another important development is the ability to look at your pictures right away—or, more importantly, for your wife to look at your pictures right away. The combination of all of these factors, plus the surprise discovery that a professional photographer would cost upwards of a hundred dollars, led me to the decision to take the damn pictures in this book myself."

ACKNOWLEDGEMENTS

I must first of all thank my parents—my mother for teaching me to look for the good in people and my father for preventing me from being tall. I should also thank my Uncle Bob, who was an early example of what the term "house arrest" means. I also thank my brother, who was my best friend until he got married and had Harold.

I should mention two Canadian icons who've been influential in my life: Pierre Berton and Stephen Leacock. Stephen Leacock for his ability to grow facial hair and Pierre Berton for his wit.

I've had many facets to my life and show business career, and my wife, Bernice, has always been the first person to support me, financially and psychologically, and even after all these years of marriage is still willing to accept my apologies.

I picked up my singing style by copying three of the great black singers of America: Louis Armstrong, Redd Foxx and Moms Mabley. I owe most of my acting technique to Hammy Hamster, who taught me two important lessons: if you're good, people can hear what you're thinking, and spend as much of your life as possible on all fours.

For my ability to take on handyman projects, I would like to thank OHIP, and socialized medicine in general. It's the only thing that kept our show on budget.

I want to mention my nephew Harold, without whom I may have been tempted to leave Possum Lodge and go out into the real world, where I would have met with frustration and disappointment. He made all of that possible without the travelling.

And lastly, I have to acknowledge all the great Red Green fans and Possum Lodge members who have allowed me the privilege of being what some would call a relentless idiot, but which I prefer to describe as a misguided genius.

Quando Omni Flunkus Mortati.

Red Green